Do you want to add a g

Read the story of M

For many years I have observed him closely. He leads the pack when it comes to underpromising and overperforming.

His quiet achievements have influenced beneficially thousands of people not only in America but also in nations overseas. I know this for a fact.

I think it was the famous evangelist Dwight L. Moody who said, "I would rather put one hundred men to work than to do the work of one hundred men."

Mr. Pursell is a master of this. One of the things that makes him unique derives from the fact that he motivates people to want to do what he knows needs to be done. I consider that nothing less than pure genius.

As I write these lines I have just returned from a prominent extended trip where I saw firsthand the multiplying power of Mr. Pursell. Specifically, it was a subtle move made that generated a pledge of more than $1.5 million for the Lord's work.

If I had one hundred heads and each head had one hundred mouths and each mouth had one hundred tongues, I could not adequately express my evaluation of this amazing man.

You will find this book, ably written by Harold Fickett, a page-turner. You'll want to underline certain passages for future referral. You'll want underlying sentences to use in your own discussions and speeches.

I congratulate Harold Fickett on this biographical tour de force. Though the life of Mr. Pursell cannot be confined within the parameters of written expression, Harold comes close to it.

Apply the principles of Mr. Pursell and enjoy an added success dimension to your life. I guarantee it!

John Edmund Haggai, author of *Success Secrets of the Bible*

An interesting account of Jim Pursell, innovator, change agent, Christian, visionary, benefactor, husband, father, the consummate role model. In a time when so many instances of executive misconduct are being publicized in the media, it is refreshing to learn about how Jim Pursell's conversion to Christian principles influenced his management style and resulted in the explosive growth of a small, family-owned farm fertilizer company into a major, comprehensive, innovative industry leader.

Achilles Armenakis, James T. Pursell Eminent Scholar,
Auburn University

If you ever had to have one friend in your life, Jimmy Pursell would be the man. He and I have been friends since high school, and I've never had a better friend. He and his wife, Chris, have always been there for me and I for them.

Jim Nabors, Entertainer (as interpreted from
scanned photo of handwritten note)

In the early days of the Fellowship of Companies for Christ, Jimmy was one of the guys I looked up to. He was creative and had a simple wisdom and was willing to share the good and the bad with young folks like me who were striving to get to where he was. He encouraged people and built a multimillion-dollar business from fertilizer, but more importantly, he impacted people for Christ through his business. This book tells the story of a man who ministered as he went along the way.

Robert L. Mitchell, Founder and Chairman of the Board

FINDING THE ULTIMATE MULTIPLIER

THE STORY OF JIMMY PURSELL

FINDING THE ULTIMATE MULTIPLIER

THE STORY OF JIMMY PURSELL

Keys to His Success in Life and Business

By Harold Fickett

The Ultimate Multiplier. . . the Key to Success to Life and Business: The Jimmy Pursell Story

First edition, June 2015

Library of Congress Control Number: 2015902463

ISBN: 978-0-578-16266-9 (hc)
ISBN: 978-0-578-16267-6 (sc)
ISBN: 978-0-578-16268-3 (e)

Printed in the United States of America

Cover photo by Michael Clemmer
Jacket Design by Tim Spanjer

TABLE OF CONTENTS

FOREWORD

It's a warm June day as I sit here at Pursell Farms. I'm sitting on the porch of Chris and Jim Pursell's house and looking across the pastures and over the golf course. So many memories are stirred as I think about this book, *The Ultimate Multiplier*, about Jim Pursell and of course Chris and the family. I think back to when I first met Jim in May 1976. I was introduced to Jim by his oldest child, Taylor. We had about four hours to talk that day. We had a great visit, and then I went on to a meeting in Birmingham. That was the beginning of a change of life for me, and since that time, I've seen many lives influenced and changed because of the life of Jimmy Pursell. As you read *The Ultimate Multiplier*, you will see so many things that have been indicative of Jim's life. Let me urge you to please read between the lines and try to place yourself in this man's skin.

Ultimate means the best, the top, you don't get any better than that—you have reached it. Jim would be the first one to recognize that only by the grace and strength of God, through Christ, has he been able to do and continue to do ultimate multiplication. On August 1 of 1976, Jim Pursell openly and publicly made a commitment of his business and a recommitment of his life to Christ.

Through the years Jim Pursell has asked two questions of me. Number one, what can I do more? And number two, what do we need to do to help more people? These are some of the things that I have seen and continue to see God doing in and through Jim Pursell. His compassion has certainly borne the burdens of many people and has thereby demonstrated mercy.

I've never seen anyone more concerned when someone has been in trouble. Jim is always there to see how he can help. This shows so much about his caring mind and heart. His caring for his wife, children, grandchildren, great-grandchildren, friends, and all who are connected to his businesses exemplifies a tremendous life of giving. Jim is a great steward of what God has given him and others.

Through the years that I've known Jim, he's been such a great encouragement to me and countless others. In 1976 he made it possible for me to leave the business world and start speaking full-time. I haven't kept up with the number of times I've spoken for Jim's company or for customers and friends of his. Every time I've been encouraged and have had the privilege to encourage others because of Jim's support. He is a great servant, defined as person who gets excited about making someone else successful. Jim has always been excited about seeing others succeed. If you take all these qualities about Jim, and there are many more, they can be wrapped up in one word: LOVE.

Jim Pursell is a great example of what Christ can do and is doing in someone who loves the Lord and loves people. With his example, may we all be encouraged to be ultimate multipliers. Ephesians 2:8–10 says, "For it is by grace you have been saved, through faith; and that not of yourselves, it is the gift of God; not as a result of works, so that no one may boast; For we are His workmanship, created in Christ Jesus for good works, which God prepared beforehand so that we would walk in them."

John S. Riley, inspirational speaker and humorist

James Taylor Pursell Sr.—known throughout his life as "Jimmy"—was born July 3, 1930, to a family of modest means in Talladega, Alabama. His father, Howard, was the principal of a local school, and Jimmy's mother, Eunice, was one of the teachers. In fact, Howard Pursell seems to have hired the future Mrs. Pursell with romance in mind.

Nothing in his background suggested that Jimmy would live a life of such significance that it could serve anyone, especially those in business, as a model for how to fulfill one's destiny.

Nothing suggested that one day he would transform a local Alabama family business into a global industry leader; help reform governance in the state of Alabama; serve as a key figure in an international movement of Christian business executives; and inspire others to pursue innovative technologies in the fight against world hunger.

There are people like Benjamin Franklin and Albert Schweitzer who start planning for greatness early in life. Jimmy Pursell's one grand dream, which passed almost as quickly as it was conceived, came at the end of his college years, when he thought of spending his life in the Air Force and one day becoming a general. Through his formative years and well beyond, he aimed at nothing much grander than securing a good job and raising a family. Even as Jimmy began to accomplish so much—to become a success by anyone's reckoning—he hardly thought about personal achievement.

There is a secret to the life of Jimmy Pursell. It's not talent, although Jimmy possessed more natural gifts than he understood as a young person or would ever be willing to admit. The secret does not lie in the connections he made, either, albeit he made a brilliant marriage, with his father-in-law setting him up in business. The time in which he lived and the way life changed in his native Alabama were more suited to making him a pauper than a rich man, since the cotton business—the original revenue driver of the family business—would soon diminish in the state.

The secret in Jimmy's life took his talents and opportunities and multiplied them exponentially. Nearly everyone looks for how this can happen in his or her own life. Everyone in business certainly looks for ways to multiply return on investment.

Jimmy discovered the "ultimate multiplier."

It was not an invention, a technique, or a set of personal or business practices. It was not any of the habits of highly effective people that are advanced, recycled, and endlessly reconfigured in self-help books.

The secret Jimmy discovered was not of his own invention. It was utterly counterintuitive. It involved risks that Jimmy thought might destroy what he had labored so hard to build, and it was not understood, at first, by most of those around him.

To this day it's not something that Jimmy can articulate well, at least in its whys and wherefores.

Nevertheless, it's at the very center of Jimmy's story, which is the reason for telling that story and finding that same ultimate multiplier for us.

The Talladega Tiger football team raced through the stadium's gate and began to circle the field as their fans let go full-throated yells, rang cowbells, and made the stands thunder by jumping up and down. The men still tailgating in the parking lot leaned on the horns of their Plymouths. Crimson-and-white-uniformed Tigers kept coming and coming. The captains in the lead had run around the field and back to the home side bench before the last of the home team players entered. Talladega High fielded as many as one hundred twenty players for its home games in the late 1940s, as WWII veterans returned to complete their high school educations. Fourteen-year-old freshmen and nineteen-year-old combat veterans suited up together as the religion of football gave the Baptist church a run for its money in the South.

The fourth game of the 1947 season saw the Tigers meeting their traditional rivals, the Sylacauga Aggies, on a still-muggy early October Saturday afternoon with dust in the air from the area's exhausted, red-dirt cotton fields.

The Tigers were on a twenty-one-game winning streak, which began on September 21, 1945. They saw future Georgia Tech All-Americans like Johnny Hicks and Glen Turner come up through their ranks, as well as

Bryant Ivey, who made his name playing basketball at Alabama. The older players gave them a front line that averaged over two hundred pounds, like a college team.

Among their offensive weapons was the Tigers' scatback, Jimmy Pursell, at five feet seven inches tall and one hundred forty-five pounds, a David among the Goliaths. They called him "Little Jimmy" and "Twinkletoes," because in a glimmer he was off and gone. He ran the 100-yard dash in under ten seconds—the world record at the time was 9.4, set by Jesse Owens.

The game that afternoon turned on a play that would keep playing out in Jimmy Pursell's life ever after. The Tigers ran the single-wing offense, the ball hiked to any one of three different players, with fake hand-offs, quick laterals, and reverses varying a constant running attack. No one threw the ball much then.

On third down and four yards to go at the Tiger's own forty-three yard line, the halfback lateraled the ball out to Jimmy, who headed around right end. Just as he planted his left foot to turn upfield, with his spikes buried deep in the turf, the opposing defensive tackle laid out and speared Jimmy's lower leg with his helmet. The whole stadium heard the crack like a pistol's report and felt the jolt down their spines. Not far down from Jimmy's kneepad, white bone arrowed through the flesh, pointing backwards to the way he had come.

Jimmy's father stood up and instantly started toward the field, his knees pistoning as he came down the steps out of the stands. A big man, heavy-set, he didn't stop at the hurricane fence surrounding the field but leapt right over it, a site that stunned his neighbors nearly as much as his son's injury.

A growing scrum of players quickly surrounded Jimmy, and the ambulance, when it finally arrived, had to turn on its siren to get close enough for its crew to load Jimmy on a litter into the back.

One of its stars gone, Talladega lost to Sylacauga that day, ending the streak—which is still the longest in the school's history.

The injury put Jimmy into the hospital for a few days and the leg, once it had been painfully reset, into a full cast. It made him more of a local celebrity than previous accounts in the newspaper of his heroics as a scatback. Groups of well-wishers gathered almost non-stop around his bed, ambassadorial parties that included the rival Sylacauga football coach and a group of popular kids from Sylacauga High School led by Jim Nabors, a tall, gangly youth with a sweep of brown hair falling into his eyes and an "aw' shucks" grin that soon enough made him famous as Gomer Pyle on Andy Griffith's television show.

So many came to visit Jimmy Pursell in the hospital that the staff confined him to a "no visitors" section and called his parents at the earliest opportunity to inquire whether it might now be convenient to have their son recuperate at home. The hospital was desperate to get all the kids out of their halls!

Teenagers become popular among their peers for all kinds of reasons, but Jimmy's popularity stemmed from a distinct combination of traits: he was outgoing, genuinely liked other people, and unassuming. He wasn't the bad boy; he was a good guy, and he was liked for being good. Truly a rare breed among teenagers.

Jimmy came from a well-educated family that grappled with the world as they found it. Both his parents were graduates of Jacksonville State Teachers College. His father's first job out of college was as a school principal. When he had the chance, he hired a young woman he had his eye on as a teacher, who soon enough became Mrs. Pursell.

Nevertheless, the Pursells' early success in education did not equate to financial stability. Principal Pursell could not make enough money in education to support a family properly, so he transitioned into selling Ford automobiles before finishing out his working life as part of county government. One of his friends from Talladega asked him into the business, which is how the Pursells made their home there. Many men would be embittered by the necessity of taking a job they could've had without the trouble of getting a college degree, but if Jimmy's father felt disappointed, his practicality soon won out over his pride.

Jimmy inherited his outgoing personality from his father, who drew people to him with lively conversation, not showing off his education but drawing upon it to everyone's delight. He took a prominent part in the

First Baptist Church of Talladega, often making the week's announcements and leading the prayer before the preacher's sermon.

Jimmy's mother, who was more retiring, loved to play the piano. She left teaching when Jimmy's older sister, Dot, was born.

Jimmy's arrival in the family five years later occasioned rejoicing, even on Dot's part. She immediately became his protector. Protection proved vital on at least one occasion when, early in the family's life together, during a brief period of residence in Shocco Springs, a rattlesnake crawled into Jimmy's crib. His mother snatched up her precious newborn before any harm could be done. In Greek literature, escaping death in infancy frequently signals a character's heroic destiny. Jimmy's mother took this as an omen that the house was no place for their family, and she had them out of there by nightfall.

When Jimmy recuperated sufficiently to return to high school, the hard cast that covered his entire leg presented obstacles. He could no longer walk to school. His father bought him an old Model A, a car that in its dozen or more years on the road had evidently seen lively times, as it had two footprints impressed into the ceiling fabric above the back seat. In his rigid cast, Jimmy still couldn't drive the car, and he had to be chauffeured back and forth from high school like a dignitary or potentate. Was he tempted to clinch a cigarette holder in his jaw and wave to the crowds like FDR? It's not hard to imagine, even for the unassuming Jimmy Pursell.

His English class met on the second floor of the high school building, and Jimmy was unable to climb stairs—that's how fragile his leg remained while on the mend. Zora Ellis, Talladega's legendary English teacher, for whom the town's junior high school is now named, told Jimmy he had been granted a reprieve from English studies. By virtue of his gridiron bravery he would be given a B in English for the balance of the year. Jimmy jokes that's the highest grade he made in high school.

That's unlikely, of course, but it does indicate how different high school once was in America. This was well before college became a universal necessity, standardized exams (the SAT and ACT) started to count as much as a diploma, and students began taking as many AP classes as possible to demonstrate the rigor of their course selections. In the years immediately following World War II, entering college required showing up and paying the modest bill. It was free for vets. Jimmy admits he had no idea in high school what he wanted to do with his life and felt fortunate that his parents' love of education spurred him to enroll at Auburn University. He majored in business because he didn't know what else to major in. At least he knew something about business through the part-time job he held in high school as a soda jerk. He knew about the demands of sheer physical labor too, as he also worked for the county engineering department, building roads and bridges, and for the city paving streets. His earnings helped put him through college.

At Auburn, Jimmy was too small to play football but he went out for track. The broken leg cost him a step, and while he no longer quite had the phenomenal speed he enjoyed in high school, Jimmy stayed in shape and enjoyed the camaraderie of his teammates.

He turned to other types of "running," as well, mostly with his fraternity brothers and that fellow he met in the hospital from Sylacauga, Jim Nabors. Jim attended the University of Alabama in Tuscaloosa. Tuscaloosa is to the west of Birmingham and Auburn to the southeast, with Sylacauga about halfway in between. They began meeting up for double dates, with Jim Nabors often persuading both girls to join them for the evening.

Typecasting truly is a cruel fate, because while the public knows Jim Nabors as everyone's favorite village idiot, the shade tree mechanic from the Andy Griffith television show, Jim Nabors impressed his peers and their parents as well as being Sylacauga's favorite son. They vied for the opportunity to entertain him in their homes. Nabors came from a modest home himself, where the cupboard was likely empty and stomachs, not the table, groaned. Students walked home for lunch, and Jim was known to choose his menu by following the trail of the most enticing aroma coming from the neighborhood, as he could always count on a welcome—anywhere, at any time.

Jimmy simply knew Nabors as an increasingly good friend, until one night they sped off with their dates to the infamous Phenix City, a town just north of Columbus, Alabama, close to the Georgia state line known for its honky-tonks and gambling. Jim Nabors and his date took over the dance floor of one place and then another and one after that. Jim was jitterbugging as if he didn't have a bone in his body, and people stood back and watched, open-mouthed, gaping, and then cheering. That was nothing because then Jim Nabors began to sing! He was a one-man show, jeep-jiving one moment and then crooning to the collective sighs of the ladies the next. Jimmy Pursell did not know quite what was happening, except that he was having the time of his life.

When he looked up to see the time, he saw what an "after-hours" club meant: it was 3 a.m.

The car carrying Pursell, Nabors, and their giddily exhausted dates crawled over the hill into Sylacauga about dawn. They went by a police cruiser on the lookout. It slid out of its concealed position and trailed them into town. No lights, no siren, just the black and white in the rearview mirror. Jim Nabors's dad was the town policeman behind them.

Pursell and Nabors survived that escapade and went on to others. Sylacauga's collective open door to their favorite son soon opened a door to Jimmy's destiny as well. They were together in Sylacauga one evening preparing for a night on the town—or trying to. Pursell had left his shaving kit at Auburn and needed to clean up before going out. Jim Nabors had a bright idea. How would Jimmy like to try one of the new electric razors? Judy Parker's father had one. Mr. Parker, a former mayor, was one of Sylacauga's most prominent businessmen; his business included cotton ginning, seed production, bale storage in bonded warehouses, and fertilizer manufacture. All in all, he served farmers within a fifty-mile radius as a vendor, business agent, and even financier. Nabors just thought they could go in and use the razor, whether or not the Parkers were home.

When Nabors and Pursell knocked on the Parkers' door, no one answered, so Nabors led Jimmy through the unlocked door down the hallway, right into Mr. Parker's bathroom, where the electric razor went buzz and the shaving commenced. When they peeked out the door to see if anyone had noticed their presence, they saw a striking girl walking down the hall toward them; she was petite but feisty and powerful. With every step she rose on her tiptoes, springing forward toward Jimmy too fast for comfort. This girl didn't so much turn his head as set it spinning. Was this Judy?

"Chris," Nabors said. "This is Chris, Jimmy, Judy's sister. Say hello."

Jimmy and Chris stood facing one another, mute.

"Or you could just stand there being embarrassed. Say hello, numbskull. What are you, like, a junior now, Chrissy?"

"A senior."

"Chris Parker, a senior at Sylacauga High, meet Jimmy Pursell, a senior at Auburn."

"I know who he is," Chris said. "He's the boy whose leg was broken."

"That was a while ago," Jim said.

"I was there. Everybody was."

"Not looking like you do now," Nabors said.

Jimmy Pursell and Chris Parker blushed simultaneously, and the romance had begun.

About that meeting, Chris would later say, "He was so cute! And he was a jock—but that wasn't even a word then."

Jimmy Pursell and Chris Parker quickly became serious about their future together. They would date steadily over the next years, as Chris finished high school and entered Mary Baldwin College in Virginia. Jimmy thought Chris the cutest girl he had ever seen and liked her feisty attitude and adventuresome spirit. She was ready to take on the world, loved a good time, and was fiercely loyal. She added dazzle to Jimmy's abilities and friendliness. Chris sensed immediately that Jimmy was a man like her father—someone she could count on who would prove smarter than anybody knew. She liked that combination. It was like a secret that they shared, one she treasured.

With marriage in his future, Jimmy began to think seriously about "how he was going to support this girl." The outbreak of the Korean War in 1950 determined his near-term plans and gave rise to thoughts of a long-term military career. Jimmy told his father-in-law that he hoped to become a general.

While in college, Jimmy had already become a member of the National Guard. In 1951 Congress passed the Universal Military Training and Service

Act that put the military draft back into overdrive. Jimmy received a deferment for his senior year at Auburn, but he would be called to service after graduation. Like nearly 1.5 million other patriotic Americans during those years, Jimmy chose his preferred means of service, enlisting in the Air Force.

As a college graduate, Jimmy was officer material, and he entered the Air Force Cadet program. Chris and he would have liked to marry right away upon his graduation from Auburn, but Cadets were not allowed to marry until they received their commission—although Jimmy found out during his training that about half his class was already married.

Jimmy was trained as a bombardier/navigator on T-29s. He learned how to go up into the bell of the airplane at night and navigate by the stars with a sextant, even while bouncing up and down in choppy air. He also practiced with the machine gun mounted in those glass domes, shooting the moon and stars. For the most part Jimmy ended up flying on C-119s, but he also trained on B-25s. In that plane the bombardier slid under the control panel in front of the pilot down into position over the bomb bay doors from where he controlled the plane as they dropped sand bombs on training runs. On B-25s the bombardier had a second station up in the nose where he commanded a machine gun.

In the early summer of 1953, Jimmy reached Mather Air Force Base just outside of Sacramento, California. There he received his commission and became a 2nd Lieutenant. Chris and Jimmy were at last able to marry, and they did so on July 10, 1953, in the base chapel. Only a handful of people were in attendance, among them Mr. and Mrs. Parker and their only son, Howard Jr., who was then eleven years old. They drove to California in a new Dodge sedan with the spare tire in a donut-holder on the back and left the car as their wedding present to the couple. Jim Nabors drove up from Los Angeles, where he was starting his career in entertainment, to serve as best man. He would drive the Parkers back to Los Angeles for their flight home.

Jimmy and Chris honeymooned at nearby Lake Tahoe and celebrated as well in the casinos of "The Biggest Little City in the World," Reno, Nevada, just over the state line from Tahoe. Theirs was a wedding and a new marriage shadowed by the specter of war. Jimmy's deployment to Korea was scheduled to take place the next month.

While he knew the risks and was hardly eager to leave his new bride, Jimmy felt ready to go. He felt well prepared and wanted to put his training to good use in a necessary cause. His thoughts of becoming a general one day were gone by this time, but he was ready to do his duty.

That did not mean, though, that both Jimmy and Chris were not greatly relieved when just ten days later, on July 27, 1953, the armistice was signed that ended the Korean War. Three years remained on Jimmy's hitch, but he would serve out his time in the States.

The military provided wonderful opportunities for Jimmy and even did a lot for Jimmy and Chris's marriage. They lived in small but comfortable housing on the bases to which Jimmy was assigned, first at Mather in Sacramento and then in Waco and Houston, Texas. Jimmy was twenty-three years old at his marriage and Chris only nineteen. Other than her year and a half at Mary Baldwin, Chris had never lived away from Sylacauga, Alabama. Her father was a commanding figure, and Jimmy, in truth, was still as much a boy as a man.

That changed in the service, though. He had the opportunity to travel to Panama and Bermuda on training missions. He ran operations on his C-119 as the loading hatch dropped and twenty-two paratroopers—eleven on each side—went out the back. He had the greatest destructive force the world has ever seen put in his hands when he was trained on how to arm the egg-shaped, trailer-truck-long nuclear bombs stored at Mather. His training for this took place in a secret facility with no notes allowed, where detailed instructions had to be committed to memory. The bombs could only be armed once out over water, so bombardiers had to protect their crews while preparing Armageddon.

Chris and Jimmy still found time to enjoy themselves and prosper in the bargain. They frequented the local officers club, where they often played bridge and usually cleaned everybody out. Bridge is all about subtle communication and numbers, knowing what your partner is trying to tell you through the way they bid, what that means about the cards they hold, how the odds are changing as bidding continues, and communicating the same in return. It's not a bad metaphor for how a marriage works. Jimmy and Chris became very good at it.

Their first son, Taylor, was born in 1954 while Jimmy was still in the service. Jimmy took a harrowing trip through Phenix City, Alabama, on the night of Taylor's birth. Jimmy's father's old roommate at Jacksonville State Teachers College, Albert Patterson, had just won the Democratic nomination for attorney general of Alabama, vowing to clean up the corruption in Phenix City, where illegal gambling fueled organized crime. He was assassinated outside his law office on June 18, 1954, and as Jimmy made his way to his wife's bedside, he was told not to stop for anything. If he had a flat, keep going!

The couple welcomed their healthy baby boy, James Taylor Pursell Jr., without incident, thankfully.

The military recognized Jimmy's abilities and made him a trainer of other bombardiers. He was well spoken and could hold trainees' attention while lecturing on technical material. Through this he grew to have a sense of authority and command; he had earned the salutes he received from those in his charge. In turn, he knew how to take orders and carry them out. He was part of a chain of command, and he grasped the chain's unifying power.

When, toward the end of his years of service, Mr. Parker asked Jimmy to return to Sylacauga and help him run his company, Jimmy could accept the offer as his own man. He was confident in his abilities, and Chris and he were secure in their marriage and family. He mustered out as a 1st Lieutenant.

CHAPTER THREE

SUPER SALESMAN

When Jimmy first went to work for his father-in-law, Howard Parker Sr., he hardly knew how to spell *fertilizer* and could not tell a cotton field from a cornfield until the bloom. He learned fast, though.

The Parker Fertilizer Company had been a family business since its founding in 1904 as the Sylacauga Fertilizer Company, Inc. Howard Parker Sr.'s father, DeWitt "Dinky" Parker, had begun the company with three other partners. He personally added both the ginning and federally bonded storage operations. His life story could have been written by Dickens, as he was orphaned by the Civil War, then fortuitously adopted by a North Carolina congressman and raised as his son. He married well too. Letitia Oden's father had a mill and at one time owned ten thousand acres between Sylacauga and Childersburg. Her father's wealth enabled Letitia to go to college, and the sale of part of her inheritance financed DeWitt's share in the fertilizer company.

DeWitt and Letitia had four children: three girls and one boy, Howard Arrington Parker. The *Arrington* came from the family who had adopted DeWitt. He did not forget how much he owed to the family who adopted him. Through the generations, this pattern of education, business acumen, and good marriages, as well as calculated entrepreneurial risks, proved a formula for prosperity. By virtue of his own marriage, they were, in a sense, Jimmy Pursell's inheritance too.

When DeWittt passed away in 1930, his son Howard left his job at the Armour Fertilizer Works in Atlanta to take over the family business. He grew up loving the land and as a teenager did some farming of his own. When he was seventeen years old, in 1913, he entered a farming contest. "I grew one hundred twenty-eight bushels of corn on my acre and got a free trip to the National Corn Exposition in Columbia, South Carolina. I also got a Berkshire male pig. When I left to go to the University of Alabama in the fall of 1914, I sold the pig to Bloise Hill for $20. I sold my corn to the Anzi-Golden Seed Company in Birmingham for $200. I also made seven hundred fifty pounds of cotton and it sold for $75." With nearly $300 in his pocket, Howard not only covered the first year's tuition and books but room and board as well.

World War I interrupted Howard's education, and he left the university for training camp in the summer of 1917. He served proudly and ever after took special care of veterans, both through the "town letters" he sent to servicemen in World War II, reporting all the latest news about Sylacauga and what he knew of its native sons serving on far-flung battlefields, and in his hiring practices. Harry Appleby Jr., after being a standout football player at Georgia Tech, became the company's longtime bookkeeper. Harry's father and Howard had served in the WWI trenches together. Howard also hired William F. "Bill" Nichols, who became a prominent executive at the company and later a US congressman. Bill's credentials included an agricultural degree and his war service, where he lost most of one leg in the fighting.

Howard's stewardship of the company was distinguished by community involvement, management practices that were at once careful and generous, a knack for marketing, and prescience as to the future of the cotton business.

Mr. Parker served on the Sylacauga City Council, the Board of Education, and was elected to mayor for one term. He had to give up that official position because of a continuing battle with tuberculosis, but he remained a political force. Anyone who knows small-town life, particularly during the period from 1930 through the 1950s, will remember how much of a town's life was in the hands of a very few men: the banker, the landholder, the dominant shopkeeper, and, like Mr. Parker, the focus of agricultural industry.

The farmers of the area essentially depended on Mr. Parker to finance their operations. He sold them their seed, their fertilizer, and even arranged for the delivery of equipment and labor. These "sales" occurred in the spring, but they were only book sales made on the basis of personal IOUs. The Sylacauga Fertilizer Company only received cash payment after Parker Gin Company processed their cotton, baled it, and helped broker it on the market. At times, because in certain years the price of cotton dropped below what farmers needed to survive, Mr. Parker stored the bales in his bonded warehouse until the price increased and the farmer could at last cash out his crop. This meant that Howard Parker sometimes carried a farmer from year to year, essentially financing the farmer's operation.

He managed the company's affairs deftly enough that in 1945 he was able to buy out all the shareholders of the Sylacauga Fertilizer Company who were not Parker descendants. (The name of the company would remain the same, however, until 1959, when it officially became the Parker Fertilizer Company.) Three years later he purchased The Southern Cotton Oil Company, opened a new fertilizer plant in 1950, and picked up three more cotton gins that expanded the area the company serviced. Far from hoarding his increasing wealth, he instituted a profit-sharing plan with the company's employees in 1954—an almost unheard-of move in that time.

Howard Parker was a deacon and central figure at the town's First United Methodist Church. In future years, as his son-in-law Jimmy Pursell set out, self-consciously, to see how far a commercial enterprise could become a "company for Christ," he thought, at least at first, that this direction represented something utterly new. And as he grew to understand the company's history more deeply, he began to appreciate just how far Mr. Parker had already gone in this direction. If Mr. Parker had not adopted the evangelical style Jimmy Pursell came to favor, Mr. Parker certainly did treat all he had dealings with in a Christlike manner.

He liked thinking up new ways to advertise his products, a trait that his grandson David Pursell would one day inherit. He once sponsored a beauty pageant and entered Miss 6/8/4—the mixture of the most popular fertilizer the company sold. Sylacauga Fertilizer Company also supported a local radio program, and Mr. Parker pressed his daughter Judy, an accomplished pianist, into entertaining the listening audience by playing for half an hour at a time. Every year when a farmer brought in his first bale of cotton, he was given a new wallet imprinted with the company's logo, and there were change purses for the ladies—a gentle and appreciated reminder of the farmer's economic lifeline. The bags of the company's fertilizer were so well made and attractive that poor people of the area made dresses for their children out of them. Mr. Parker even found a stolen shipment of the bags washed and hanging out to dry on the thief's clothesline.

What truly distinguished Mr. Parker, though, was his foresight. However generous he wanted to be in terms of supporting local farmers, he could not stop changes in the market that suggested growing cotton in the area might not be viable for long.

"I worry about our business," Mr. Parker wrote in his diary. "What will farming be like in five years, ten years? Can we make the change?"

The boll weevil and other pests were degrading crop yields, and the pesticides used against them were becoming increasingly expensive as the pests grew immune to old formulas. Synthetic fibers were reducing the need for cotton, while other countries, finally rebounding after World War II, were starting to grow their own crops with cheaper labor. The mechanization of farming was well under way. This demanded greater investments in technology, which only made sense when farming on a much larger scale than was possible in the patchwork fields of Alabama. Mr. Parker saw the future in cotton as belonging to the Louisiana delta, the high plains of Texas, and California's central valley where huge acreages could be irrigated.

Mr. Parker suggested to Jimmy that he and Chris join him in buying up many of the area cotton gins and moving them out to Texas or California to make a go of it. Or, Jimmy could take over sales for the new line of lawn and garden fertilizers that the company was producing. The year before Jimmy joined the company, in 1955, Mr. Parker had established the Sta-Green Plant Food Company. Sta-Green marketed a mixture that was a slow-release, nitrogen-based product. It did not differ fundamentally from the product that the company sold to farmers, but it was packaged in bright, polyethylene, twenty-five-pound bags and advertised as a "special formula" for camellias and azaleas. The margins were huge in lawn and garden as compared to agriculture.

Jimmy did not think much of the cotton-ginning idea. Ginning was a nasty, sweaty business, and the equipment used was prone to catching on fire. He did not think the dilapidated cotton gins dotting the landscape were worth the effort to move them.

He had already made enough sales calls for the fertilizer company to know that sales fitted his strengths. His knowledge of the area as a hometown boy, the associations he had made at Auburn University, the experience of the military he shared with so many men, his genuine appreciation for people, and his naturally outgoing personality combined to make him a super salesman. He could strike up a conversation with anybody because he enjoyed doing so. Once he got to know people, then he could figure out how his product might solve a need they had, and that made the sale.

Mr. Parker started the Sta-Green line because, as many misgivings as he had about the future of cotton in Alabama, he saw that America was growing rich. More and more families could afford their own homes and were moving into suburbs. In fact, Mr. Parker had built a subdivision himself, Capitol Drive, named for the "capitol highway" that led past the property to Montgomery. Homeowners wanted green lawns and flourishing gardens, and that meant a booming lawn and garden business in fertilizer—if they could market and sell their product effectively.

Jimmy's father-in-law saw quickly that he had made a good decision in putting the Sta-Green line in Jimmy's hands. "The big companies are fighting each other and trying to stomp out us little ones," he wrote. "But Jimmy and his Sta-Green line are doing fine. He is a natural-born salesman."

One of Jimmy's first substantial accounts was the Aldridge Garden Shop in Birmingham. Mr. and Mrs. Aldridge and their son Eddie all took a shine to Jimmy. His sales to Aldridge Garden grew right along with their business. They were smart in how they promoted it, trading plants and landscaping for television advertising time with a local station. Soon Sta-Green was shipping half truckloads to the Birmingham area.

People in the business talked about what was working for them, and that helped Jimmy open up substantial markets in Montgomery and Mobile as well. From there, Sta-Green spread to Huntsville and Atlanta and throughout the Southeast. Mr. Parker was amazed that you could take a twenty-five-pound bag of fertilizer and sell it for $5!

At the same time, Jimmy started a side business that would play a pivotal role in the future. When he came back from the service, Jimmy went into the outdoor billboard advertising business with his father. His father soon tired of it, but Jimmy was able to find another partner, actually teaming up with a former competitor. Together they founded Coosa Valley Advertising. Jimmy and his partner built up the business until they owned two hundred fifty billboards.

His involvement in advertising underlined for Jimmy that the way something is presented often has as much to do with its success as the value of the product. Sta-Green took an agricultural product and turned it into a "specialty product" for the lawn and garden market. The lawn and garden market was more diverse, though, than simply camellias and azaleas. "Specialty products" in that market could be made for virtually every type of plant. With that insight Jimmy began proliferating the product offerings of Sta-Green through packaging, labeling, sizing, and pricing. A product for every plant and in sizes that appealed to the whole range of customers.

What began through offering "specialty products" and initially based purely on marketing would not end there. What if one really could devise a different type of fertilizer for each and every type of plant? That was a question that would preoccupy Jimmy for the next fifty years and still does today.

Mr. Parker watched proudly as Jimmy and Chris settled into Sylacauga and established their family. Their second child, a daughter called Chris, or "Chrissy," after her mother, arrived soon after the family moved to Sylacauga in 1956. Their last child, David, was born April 2, 1959. Eldest son Taylor gave his maternal grandmother a whole new name, as the children and then everyone else starting calling Mrs. Ola Parker "Tree Top." Taylor would hold up his hands and ask for his grandmother to sing him a lullaby, "Tree Top, Tree Top!" As in, "Rock-a-bye baby in the *tree tops* . . ."

As America has become a more mobile society, with higher education and corporate jobs leading the next generation to move away from their childhood homes, the storyline of the Parker and Pursell clan, in which a family business sustains succeeding generations, has receded. It may seem like an anachronism belonging to the "escape from the small town" literature of Thornton Wilder and Eugene O'Neill. It's certainly not a common story any longer, even in rural America, as globalization has changed the nature of commerce. By far the greater percentage of families that had businesses like the Parkers in the 1950s and 1960s simply don't any longer. Even Parker Fertilizer would have gone out of business soon enough if not for the family's ability—indeed, their positive genius—for adapting to changing conditions.

As we have seen, Mr. Parker was concerned about the changing nature of the cotton business in the United States and how he could diversify the business so that it provided for his own family and his employees long into the future. Howard Parker's business interests not only consisted in Parker Fertilizer, but also cotton ginning and seed sales through Parker Gin Company and warehousing through Sylacauga Bonded Warehouses. The three businesses supported each other. Everything but fertilizer production and sales, however, depended on a healthy cotton market; only the fertilizer business could be adapted to a new market via the Sta-Green line.

Ironically, though, in the late 1950s and early 1960s, selling fertilizer, even as the Sta-Green line took hold and became successful, was the least lucrative part of the enterprise. The Parker family business made more money out of ginning cotton and selling the seed back to the farmers from whose cotton it had come than its other activities. Warehousing was a cash cow, with rental fees coming in on over twenty thousand bales month after month. Bill Nichols, the war hero with a Bronze Star and a Purple Heart to his credit, ran ginning and seed sales.

Nichols was a natural speaker and leader—he had been captain of the Auburn football team. During a dinner table conversation in 1958, a civic leader suggested that Bill should run for the Alabama legislature. The next day the dinner guests spread the word in town that Bill was, in fact, a candidate, which, as they hoped, turned into a self-fulfilling prophecy. Nichols was elected to the Alabama House of Representatives in 1959 and to the Alabama Senate in 1963. The Capitol Press Corps voted him the "Most Outstanding Member of the Alabama Senate" in 1965.

The future of his company and the people he loved were much on Howard Parker Sr.'s mind during the early 1960s, as his health began to fail. His own son, Howard Jr., came to manhood during this time. On August 24, 1963, Mr. Parker wrote in his diary, "This has been one of my finest days. Howard Jr. graduated from Auburn today. How proud we all are of him."

After graduation, Howard Jr. quickly joined the family business, and his father watched over his progress with great satisfaction. "Howard Jr. and Bill Nichols went to Shelby County today to sell fall fertilizer and seed. They did fine and Howard was pleased over the day's work. He is taking to our business like a duck to water and I am so pleased."

By 1963, Howard Parker probably knew he was dying. A tall man, his weight had dropped to 126 pounds, and his suits had to be recut so that he could attend his beloved Methodist Church.

He thought he had his son's future mapped out and the other members of his leadership team provided for. Two months before Howard Jr. graduated from college, Mr. Parker wrote: "Howard Jr. should learn to sell farm fertilizers and seed under the P.M.A. [Produce Marketing Association] farm program. He should learn to collect and solicit ginning for the Sylacauga and Harpersville gins. He should also have charge of the lime and fertilizer spreading. By December 1st, he can get with Bill [Nichols] and learn something about cottonseed. Jimmy [Pursell] should be made President of the Parker Fertilizer Co., Bill Nichols President of the Parker Gin Co., and Howard Jr. President of the Sylacauga Bonded Warehouse." These were wise and thoughtful plans. He would put his son over a stable source of income, and one that required the least experience and management. He planned on giving Jimmy free reign to continue the company's conversion of its fertilizer business from agriculture to lawn and garden. The man with the most experience, Bill Nichols, would attend to the company's most lucrative business. Even Jimmy knew, at that point, that his branch of the company needed the agricultural base to win its ultimate place in the lawn and garden market.

Early in 1964, on February 4, Howard Parker Sr. passed away. He was sixty-seven years old.

After Mr. Parker's death, the three men worked in an easy alliance, as Howard Jr. had always looked up to Jimmy as a big brother and Jimmy and Bill were literally next-door neighbors in a residential subdivision Mr. Parker had developed. Naturally, there was jockeying for position as each man considered the future.

Then, tragedy struck. In the spring of 1966, while calling on a customer, Howard Jr. became suddenly ill. He was taken to the hospital and an aneurysm diagnosed. He died several days later on March 26, 1966, at the age of twenty-five. He left behind his bride of two-and-a-half years, Nona Claire Pope Parker.

That spring, having been recognized as Alabama's outstanding state senator, Bill Nichols was being urged to run for Congress. He had gone to work for Mr. Parker in 1947 and had spent nearly twenty years at the company. Alabama's 3rd Congressional District was a safe, "blue dog," Democratic seat, but Nichols had to get through the primary. That meant he had to commit himself to the race early in 1966.

One of the oddities of the race proved to be Nichols's opponent, who turned out to be Jimmy Pursell's partner in Coosa Valley Advertising. With Nichols running, Jimmy decided to back him, sell his equity in the billboard business, and use the money as a down payment on a company buyout, saying, "If I was going to devote my life to the company, I wanted to be my own boss and do my own thing."

As Bill Nichols went off to Congress, where he would serve for the next twenty-two years, Jimmy became the sole owner of Parker Fertilizer and its related businesses, acquiring shares owned by his sister-in-law, Julia (Judy) Parker McDonald, of Montgomery.

Certainly, the loss of Mr. Parker and Howard Jr. were keenly felt, but the late 1960s and early 1970s were good years for the Pursell family. The Sta-Green product line continued to grow rapidly, more than replacing the revenues generated by cotton ginning, seed sales, and even warehousing, as Mr. Parker had the wisdom to foresee. In 1978, when the Parker Gin Company burned to the ground during a police-and-firemen's strike in Sylacauga, Jimmy decided not to rebuild, a decision which ended ginning and storage operations.

The pattern of life at the Pursell household followed the familiar model of the time. Jimmy worked long, long hours. He was forever on the phone keeping in touch with accounts, assessing the business climate with others in the business, and taking particular pleasure in getting the best possible pricing on commodities. He never used pressure tactics exactly. He would simply keep talking in the friendliest way imaginable until the filibuster resulted in the price he wanted. He did break away from the office on special occasions, and the three Pursell children remember times with their dad at Auburn football games and weeks spent at their summerhouse on Lake Martin.

The children's mother, Chris Pursell, kept everyone in line. Her favorite method of quelling temper tantrums was to pour a pitcher of water on a child's head. She's still prone to knuckle up her fist and give you a friendly talking to if you don't buckle your seat belt or pay sufficient attention to nutrition.

None of the kids had any doubt about the family nature of the company, as all three worked in different capacities at their family's business while growing up. Jimmy did not forget his time working for the county on roads and bridges or paving Sylacauga's streets. He wanted his children, especially his boys, to experience real labor and how labor translated into the value of a dollar. With Jimmy, even his kids had to earn their wings.

The eldest child, Taylor, was entrepreneurial from the beginning and started working at the company at age twelve, shoveling cottonseed at the gin after school. At fourteen years old, he had the chance to earn more money by stacking bags of fertilizer, a job that had the side-benefit of helping with his football conditioning. The next year he was supervising the bone meal crew. His wild streak came out when he told the five African-American women shoveling with him that the meal was made up of "ground-up people." He must have said it with authority because they screamed, threw down their shovels, and ran away never to return. Word of this spread to such a degree that plant manager Joe Roberson could hardly find replacement workers. That was the end of Taylor's supervisory career—at least for the time being.

Chrissy hardly weighed as much as one of the fertilizer bags, so she spent her time filling bottles with water-soluble fertilizer and working in the office at administrative tasks. With an outgoing personality like her father, she later transitioned into sales, traveling the state of Alabama.

Where Taylor had a wild streak, David was stubborn. He could resist direction but then turn around and be utterly tenacious in accomplishing the same task—notably, when he failed algebra the first go-round in high school and then made As in both the basic and advanced classes. Like Taylor, David started at age twelve moving piles of cottonseed. Later, he worked in the small-package department, packing fertilizer after school and on weekends.

Far from spoiled, the Pursell children do not recall any great sense of growing up in a privileged family partly because they were required to work for their spending money and partly because the greater part of their family's success still lay in the future.

When David recalls his parents enjoying themselves, he remembers late summer afternoons on Lake Martin. His father had already tired all the kids out by driving the motorboat and taking them water skiing. Then Chris and he would take out a day-sailor and glide over the lake as the sun went down to enjoy a smoke, a cocktail, and one another's company. There were at least a few lazy days like this for Chris and Jimmy but not many.

In the late 1960s and early 1970s, Jimmy began pursuing ways to improve the Sta-Green product and increase market share. Advances in "controlled-release" products were coming along. DuPont made a bright yellow product called Uramite, and the Hercules Product Company followed with "Blue-Chip." It was almost impossible to burn plants with these products, and they lasted ten times longer than the hand-mixtures that Parker Fertilizer began with.

In 1973, Jimmy was reading a trade journal when he came on an article about the Tennessee Valley Authority (TVA) experimenting with a new type of fertilizer, Sulfur Coated Urea (SCU). If the process could be perfected, the sulfur coating would extend the life of the fertilizer over a greatly expanded time period, eliminating the need for repeated applications and guarding against fertilizer burn. Jimmy was intrigued and picked up the phone.

Jimmy and his team soon visited the TVA's Sulfur Coated Urea plant in Muscle Shoals, Alabama, to collect information on its possible advantages. While SCU might be more expensive initially, Jimmy thought, the longevity of an SCU application would make the new technology more economical for the consumer in the long run as well as provide superior performance. The margins for this product would be greater and the chance to be among its first suppliers to consumers could gain Parker significant market share—not merely regionally but nationally. This was an enormous prospect for a family-owned company in Sylacauga, Alabama.

If SCU worked, that is. The process involved spraying molten sulfur to do the coating. The first sulfur coatings had a tendency to crack, and the fertilizer would spoil in its packaging. Eventually, TVA solved that problem.

Jimmy's Parker Fertilizer Company was on the scene early enough that they were able to run tests with consumers and verify that SCU technology produced a fertilizer product vastly superior to anything on the market.

When TVA went into production in 1974, Parker Fertilizer bought the first rail car load produced. The transformation of Parker Fertilizer from a local to a national and possibly international company had begun.

For several years, Sta-Green and its chief competitor, Vigoro, dominated the lawn and garden market with their SCU products. Major retailers came on board, Lowe's, Wal-Mart, and others. Orders for half a truckload turned into orders for railroad cars stuffed to the brim. Parker bought about half the SCU tonnage TVA produced.

From the mid- to late-1970s, four companies were chiefly packaging and distributing the TVA's SCU product. They all began looking at manufacturing the product themselves and began lobbying Congress that it wasn't right for the TVA to be in competition with private businesses. They won this political battle, and the TVA was force to cede SCU technology to private industry.

Jimmy wanted to begin manufacturing SCU fertilizer immediately, but his original plans for a partnership to construct a manufacturing plant fell through. Parker Fertilizer could only buy SCU from a third-party supplier, which limited the company's profitability.

CHAPTER FIVE
THE KICKOFF

In the same time period in which Parker Fertilizer began employing new technology, changes were taking place within Jimmy's family that would have an even greater impact on Jimmy's life and eventually his company.

In 1972 Taylor Pursell graduated from high school and matriculated at Auburn University, where he studied commercial art and marketing.

During his four years at Auburn, Taylor Pursell encountered a phenomenon known as "Rat's" and the man behind it, John "Rat" Riley. John had only recently graduated from Auburn University himself in 1970, where he had been a football hero. Playing under the legendary Auburn coach, Ralph "Shug" Jordan, John Riley was named to the All-Southeastern Conference Scholastic Team in 1968 and 1969 and was named an All-American in 1970. He was a place kicker. While he now claims that he "could kick it a long way, even if [he] had no idea of where it was going," his record says differently. He still ranks eighth in all-time career scoring at Auburn University, with the second-longest field goal in history, a fifty-six-yarder made against Tennessee in 1969. Over the course of his career he made thirty-one fields goals and eighty PATs. During his high school years, Taylor would have seen Riley's heroics many times, as the Pursells were regulars at Auburn home games.

Riley was brought up in the Protestant faith and religion had always been part of his life. Now the person of Jesus Christ simply was his life—all of it. Or he aspired to give himself as completely as he could to God. (Sainthood is a process.)

An All-American football player who undergoes a conversion experience always attracts attention and even becomes controversial, as we've seen with Tim Tebow recently. John Riley was soon invited to speak about his conversion, and he discovered that he enjoyed speaking and had a knack for it. Every time he spoke he wanted to do it again. His audiences always wanted to hear more as well, and long before he graduated from Auburn he was speaking three or four times a week.

Riley's speaking gift consists in the sense of ease he conveys, his baritone voice—a radio announcer's rather than a preacher's—and the speed with which he can go from light, self-effacing humor to a depth of feeling that's unmistakably genuine. His audiences feel they know John after they hear him, and they are pretty much right, as he's rarely less than candid. That's part of his appeal too.

After his conversion the only thing that competed for John's devotion was football. Drafted by the Oakland Raiders, John Riley headed for training camp and made it to the last cut before being asked for his playbook. His future Hall of Fame member coach, John Madden, told John that leaving football would bring better things into his life. It was a shocking thing for Madden to say, and a word that a disappointed John Riley had a hard time believing. But it was one that would quickly prove true.

John Riley went to work recruiting workers as a member of the human resources department of the West-Point Pepperell, Inc., a local textile manufacturer. These were the years of the "Jesus Movement," and enthusiastic Bible studies were springing up on college campuses. The University of Alabama had a large and growing Bible study, and not to be outdone, some University of Auburn alumni contacted John to see if he would lead a Bible study on campus. There wasn't any pay involved, but that didn't matter to John.

John was smart enough to use his recruiting skills both to boost attendance at the study and to minimize his own workload. He attracted good-looking and talented students from fraternities and sororities to handle organization, music, and marketing. The core of popular students he attracted brought in many others, and the Bible study grew from a handful to more than seven hundred fifty, crowding out the biggest lecture hall at Auburn. The fire chief was willing to turn a blind eye to the overcrowded conditions because he trusted John and embraced what he was doing.

It was during John Riley's time at Auburn that Taylor underwent a conversion to Christianity that directed all his future endeavors. He became enthralled with the person of Jesus Christ and the central idea of Christian discipleship, exchanging one's own life for Christ's eternal life.

In "Rat's"—John Riley's Bible study—Taylor Pursell encountered a different type of Christianity than what he had known growing up. It would be a mistake to suppose that Jimmy and Chris Pursell had neglected the religious education of their children. They attended the Episcopal Church faithfully and participated in the congregation's leadership. As Taylor became ever more enthusiastic about Christianity and brought his enthusiasm home, his mother, Chris, resented Taylor acting as if the Pursell family did not know the true meaning of Christianity.

We have arrived at one of the central mysteries of Jimmy Pursell's story and that of his family. They lived a good, moral life, and Christianity was certainly part of that life. Jesus Christ was not the sum and substance of their lives, though, not in the way Christ had become for John Riley and not in the way that Taylor Pursell was coming to understand Christianity through John. There's sometimes a fine line between cultish fanaticism and the type of commitment Jesus demands when he says that unless a man is willing to leave father and mother and possessions too, he is not worthy to enter the kingdom of heaven. We have a tendency to domesticate Christianity, assign it a compartment in our lives, and attend to our faith as required or in times of distress. The all-demanding nature of taking up one's cross and following Christ, though, has always been the mark of the type of Christians who have changed history—from the apostle Paul to St. Francis to William Wilberforce to Billy Graham. John Riley was that type of Christian, and Taylor was deciding he wanted to be one too.

Much to his credit, Jimmy Pursell kept his own counsel as he watched what was happening in Taylor's life. Apart from Taylor's occasional insensitivity to his mother, Jimmy liked the changes he was seeing, and he loved his son so much it made him wonder about John Riley and whether there wasn't something in John Riley's approach that he needed to adopt as well.

Taylor Pursell's friendship with John Riley progressed in a way that John Riley would always find endearing and amusing. After one session of the Bible study ended, Taylor approached John, shot out his hand, and said, "I'm Taylor Pursell."

"Nice to meet you, Taylor," John said.

After the next Bible study, Taylor came up once again. "I'm Taylor Pursell," he said.

"Yes, Taylor," John said. "I remember."

After the next Bible study concluded, Taylor approached again. "Taylor Pursell," he said.

By this time, John figured Taylor must have something on his mind. "Do you want to ask me a question, Taylor?"

"Is this what you do?" Taylor asked. "Are you paid to do this?"

John told the young man about his job at West Point-Pepperell and that he taught the Bible study as a volunteer.

These after-Bible-study meetings continued until one day Taylor said, "I think you should meet my father." Riley guessed Taylor wanted him to witness to his father, which was fine with John, and he agreed to fit in a meeting with Taylor's father in conjunction with a future speaking engagement.

At Christmas, Taylor and another friend gave John Riley a suit and everything needed to go with it: a dress shirt, a tie, cufflinks, and a belt—everything but shoes. John Riley had never received a gift like that before and certainly not from Auburn undergraduates. He was grateful but didn't know entirely what to think. Taylor claims that the suit was probably purchased at Goodwill, but John remembers it as quite a nice suit and one he wore for a long time to come.

In the early spring of 1976, John Riley found it convenient to stop by the Parker Fertilizer Company in Sylacauga on his way to another speaking engagement. He met the man he knew only as Taylor's father, but the two men, each in his own way a super salesman, had an instant rapport. What John anticipated would be a half-hour to an hour meeting turned into an affair that lasted most of the day—from mid-morning until the late afternoon, when John had to get back on the road to his speaking engagement. Jimmy gave John a tour through all the company's facilities, introduced him to all the key people, and toured through the neighboring Fayetteville area where Jimmy was acquiring property that would one day be called "Pennywinkle Farms." John enjoyed Jimmy's company thoroughly, albeit Jimmy's agenda for their meeting turned out to be a surprise. Jimmy talked about the changes he had seen in Taylor as a result of John's mentoring, and John explained what he believed about the Christian faith: professing that salvation lay in repenting of one's sins and asking Jesus Christ into one's life as personal Lord and Savior.

John was starting into his good-byes when Jimmy asked, "Do you like speaking?"

"You know, I do," John said. "When I speak, I find that I just want to get up and do it again. It suits me somehow."

"What if you could do it all the time?" Jimmy asked.

"I've thought about it," John said. He did not say more because he had not only thought about it but he had also been praying the past three years that God would make it possible for him to speak full-time. He had not spoken of this desire to anyone other than God. He was not going to speak about it now to Jimmy Pursell. John feared the risks entailed in leaving his good job for full-time Christian work, and he wanted to make completely sure that he did not bring about that situation in any way through his own manipulation.

"I want you to," Jimmy said. "I think you should."

"I appreciate that," John said, mystified.

"This may be the craziest thing I've ever done," Jimmy said, "but I trust my son, Taylor, and what he says about you. I'm willing to hire you as an employee and pay you a salary that will enable you to speak full-time. Of course, I'll want you to speak to our employees as well—once a week."

Riley was so surprised he asked Jimmy to repeat the offer. He needed to be sure he wasn't dreaming.

Jimmy would never know exactly why he made this offer, except he had seen what John had done for his son, Taylor, and he liked John. He also had the sense, for reasons he couldn't really articulate, that John was going to be an important person in the life of his family and his own for a long time to come. Jimmy was certainly right about that. Riley would continue to have a major influence on the family, as his daughter, Chris, and son David would also commit themselves to Christ as a result of John's teaching. John would go on being "part of the company" to this day.

During this same year, 1976, Jimmy and Chris went through their own Christian conversions—quietly and with few outward signs. Because their conversions were choices freely made in the midst of successful and happy lives, their change of heart was as subtle and difficult to detect as a flower's tracking of the rising sun.

Jimmy and Chris went to church. They believed in God and the Christian story. Like the vast majority of Christians, however, they were living compartmentalized lives. Church was something for Sundays. Business had its own set of rules. Social life, family life, community service, etc.—all these operated according to their own conventions.

Once they gave their lives to Christ, though, the walls of the various compartments came down and every facet of their lives came together, integrated. The effect was like carbon being changed into a diamond under a powerfully concentrating force, a diamond that would refract the light of Christ in every direction.

The change did not take place all at once, of course. The first things to change were personal habits. The evangelist Wales Goebel convinced the Pursells that their Christian witness would be destroyed if they continued to smoke and drink. One night Jimmy went out to the storage shed where he had rounded up all the whiskey and poured it all out down a drain—an event that caused his brother-in-law Ken Power distress. Couldn't he have given it to him?

These behavioral changes followed a typical pattern for someone "born again" in Protestant circles. While Jimmy and Chris felt strongly at the time that their witness would be compromised by smoking and drinking, they never believed such lifestyle changes were the *sine qua non* of spirituality. They respected the faith of others who felt differently.

The next step Jimmy felt led to take was far more unusual, even mystical, as Jimmy felt led to give his business to Christ. He did not know much about what this meant—the changes it would entail. He knew only that he wanted to commit himself totally to God and that his life was wrapped up in the business. So he presented it as a gift to God, to do what God willed.

He would find, as those who make sacrifices to God do, that no one can out-give God. Jimmy's son, David, says, "My father gave the thing he loved the most, his business, to God, and God blessed him." Without knowing it, Jimmy had placed his business in the hands of the Ultimate Multiplier.

At the beginning, though, the commitment seemed full of risk, without any foreseeable upside. He was afraid he was going to "ruin his company by mixing religion and business."

Nevertheless, in 1976, Jimmy assembled the entire company for an unusual presentation. He told his employees that from now on the company would be dedicated to Christ. They would treat all of their business partners, their employees, and their clients in accord with Christian principles and try to find ways to make the company of greater service, not only in the products they provided but also in using a share of the revenues for charitable and civic purposes. (The company had always been charitable, of course, but now the revenues devoted to charity would increase with a higher percentage directed into evangelism.) Then Jimmy asked John Riley to speak, who followed with the basics of the Christian gospel.

Jimmy's speech was somewhat stumbling, as he was only beginning to walk this path and hardly knew the road he had chosen. He was relieved and gratified at the response he received from the employees, however. Their only real worries, it seemed, concerned whether beer would still be served at the company picnic.

CHAPTER SIX

Spirit-Directed Business

Nixing beer at the company picnic proved simple in comparison to changing the way the company had always entertained its best customers. Even Jimmy found the idea of not offering drinks to clients a throat-swallowing concern.

Every year, in fact, Sta-Green hosted what Jimmy described to a friend as the "biggest and best cocktail party around" at the Southern Nursery Association's trade show in Atlanta. Sta-Green rented a large suite in the downtown Marriott Motor Lodge and offered an open bar to encourage salespeople to stop by and become acquainted. There were also exhibits in the convention hall where future orders were taken, but those orders were a secondary consideration at the trade show. The ongoing cocktail party facilitated lasting friendships that enabled the business to drive forward year after year.

No one ever misbehaved; that wasn't the issue, except for one gentleman who became overly attentive to a female guest. Jimmy walked him out, and the man later apologized for his behavior. Still, the biggest and best cocktail party around did not seem the best way of showcasing a company dedicated to Christ, so the format had to be changed.

The company still rented the suite, but the open bar went away and was replaced with free ice cream sundaes for the kids. In addition, the company arranged for a worship service on Sunday morning. Jimmy's son, Taylor, observed that the sale people at the trade show were still sleeping off the drink of the night before, but Jimmy's fellow CEOs and their wives showed up at the worship service. They saw to it that their salespeople continued to do business with Sta-Green, and as far as Jimmy could tell, he didn't lose a customer.

He almost lost a salesperson, though, when he received an invoice for expenses from a golf outing. One of the company's best people had not been able to resist entertaining the customers on the outing with drinks. That wasn't the way the company was going to be managed anymore; the salesman could either comply or find other employment. He apologized and stayed.

In the late winter of 1979, Jimmy received a call from a man in Atlanta named Bobby Mitchell. Mitchell was organizing a conference at the Marriott Motor Hotel that would take place in January 1980. A fellow businessman and born-again Christian, Bobby Mitchell had heard that Jimmy had hired John "Rat" Riley as his company's chaplain. He had dedicated his company to Christ, as Mitchell understood it. The proposed conference would address the issue of running a company for Christ. A nucleus of men, most of whom owned their own companies, had been exploring the question of whether a business could truly be run on Christian principles. What would that mean? Jimmy had already taken action in this direction. Would he come to the conference and give his testimony?

"What's a testimony?" Jimmy asked.

When Jimmy felt compelled to give his company to Christ he could not see far beyond the need to take a public stand, eliminate alcohol from the way the company entertained its clients, and supply spiritual counsel to his employees and fellow townsmen. The person who invited Jimmy to the conference, Bobby Mitchell, had not gone as far in practical steps, but Bobby and a group of men around him had heard the same calling to give their companies to Christ. The same inspiration had come to mind among a nexus of powerful and astute businessmen across a swath of the American southeast, from Alabama to Georgia to the Carolinas. It was as if the Holy Spirit had blown through the area like a cyclone, touching down in one place and another, leaving men all-turned-around, stunned and dazed, unable to think about anything but one fixed idea—to give their companies to Christ.

In Bobby's case, he had read Charles Sheldon's *In His Steps*, in which an evangelist challenges a congregation of merely social Christians to ask, "What would Jesus do?" One of the book's protagonists is Milton Wright, a businessman who begins doing business in a whole new way. Bobby Mitchell could not get Milton Wright out of his mind. He kept asking, "What would it be like to commit a business to God and allow Him to guide my decisions?" By the novel's end he had resolved to run a business for Christ if given the opportunity.

A trained chemical and ceramic engineer, Bobby Mitchell had joined a Fortune 100 company out of college and had run the largest refracting plant in the country as one of his company's Early Identified High Potential hotshots. His progress toward making a fortune wasn't fast enough, though, and he left the company to go into real estate.

When the economy crashed in the mid-1970s, Bobby decided to go back to his engineering roots and prayed for the chance to be another Milton Wright. He felt that if he were involved in a larger business, he "could make a greater impact so that people could grasp how a Christian business functioned."

Soon, Bert Stumberg, the owner of a chemical business called SCC, called him. Bert knew of Bobby through Georgia Tech connections, including Bobby's father, who taught there. In addition to his ownership of SCC, Bert was the chairman of the board of another, smaller company, Applied Ceramics, which was struggling to survive. He asked Bobby to do an analysis of the situation and advise the board as to whether the company deserved a capital infusion or should declare bankruptcy.

The report so impressed Bert and his fellow board members that they approached Bobby about running the company. Bobby had two stipulations: (1) that he be allowed to run the company on Christian principles, and (2) that he be given a $100,000 line of credit.

Bert and Bobby quickly became close friends. Bert approached Bobby when he felt that his son, BG, had "gone off the deep end." His son had become a Christian, and Bert feared he was becoming a fanatic. Bobby took BG to a Bible study led by a Campus Crusade man, Dan Hayes, and soon Bert was coming as well, although at the time he was fifty-three years old and most in attendance were, like Bobby and his son, twenty-five to thirty-five. The Bible study mostly addressed how to be a good husband and father and other relational issues of the Christian life. But one morning Dan Hayes erupted with hellfire and brimstone. Bert sat weeping on the couch. What Bobby did not know at the time was that Bert had once promised to serve God the rest of his days. His was a "foxhole conversion," or rather, "deathbed conversion," as a POW during World War II in Germany. Captured three times, he pled to God for his life to be spared as he was digging his own grave. Instead of being shot right at the end of the war, the Germans holding him melted away, and his life was, indeed, spared. He hadn't lived for God subsequently, however. In the Bible study, he repented and "went off the deep end" himself. Together, Bobby and Bert and their wives began attending every seminar they could find.

After his conversion, Bert's eyes lit up when Bobby spoke about running their companies for Christ. In the late 1970s, they attended studies and presentations by Christian leaders who were becoming well known throughout evangelical Christianity. They became particularly close with the leader of Crown Financial Ministries, Larry Burkett, and the leader of Walk Through the Bible, Bruce Wilkinson. They also met with Prison Fellowship's Charles Colson, Campus Crusade's Bill Bright, and another financier, Ron Blue, as well as Howard Hendricks, Pat McMillan, and Jim Bo Heiskell. They tried to get these leaders to take on the task of forming a Christian fellowship devoted to business leaders, but the idea had no appeal for them. The usually visionary Bill Bright reacted by saying that he wasn't interested, but if they got it going, Campus Crusade would be a great place to donate the money.

Bright unintentionally summed up the bifurcated thinking that separated business from the Christian life. What did one have to do with the other? For the clergy, the meaning of business came down to its charitable-giving potential. Business wasn't necessarily an evil; it just played no part in their understanding of God's kingdom.

This meant that the lives of people like Jimmy Pursell and Bobby Mithell and Bert Stumberg were devoted to something less, in every sense, than "full-time Christian ministry." They had given their lives to God, though, and they were ready to devote their businesses to Him as well. Why should they feel called to an impossible task? Why would God relegate most of their lives to the secular?

Eventually, during the late 1970s, Bobby and Bert organized a meeting to talk about this notion of running a company for Christ. Seventy were invited. Twelve came. Nine of those men committed to meeting every other week for a couple of years to investigate the concept.

The group became convinced of the idea's importance and also that no one would organize a fellowship for the purpose if the group itself did not. Bert belonged to an association of business owners he found extremely helpful. Everyone in the association had to own his own business and no member could be the direct competitor of another. The association staged three conferences a year: a one-day seminar, a two-day seminar, and a three-day seminar that took place at a resort. Bobby and Bert decided to adopt its rule of requiring members to be either a CEO or business owner and its yearly schedule of conferences. The fortnightly meetings of the small group would continue as well. The first conference held was the one to which Jimmy Pursell was invited to give his testimony—whatever a testimony was.

From the beginning of what would become the *Fellowship of Companies for Christ* there was both tremendous camaraderie among the founders and open disagreement. If the common question was, "What would Jesus do?" the answer could often be peculiar to the responder. The meetings of the small group that served as the fellowship's nucleus were often contentious, which made the spirit of unity that ultimately prevailed at meeting's end unaccountable. Everyone felt the lack, though, of a common understanding—a theology—of business.

This common understanding did not arrive until late in the summer at the Point Clear three-day conference. Walk Through the Bible's Bruce Wilkinson and his associate Walt Wiley (now president and founder of Winning with Encouragement) were the speakers. Bruce did not want to speak. He was only persuaded, it would seem, because the core group were enthusiastic supporters of his own ministry. Out of a sense of obligation he went to the library to see what he could find on the topic and prepare his talks. He found virtually nothing, and he arrived at the conference with only a few generic ideas.

Halfway through the conference, Bruce Wilkinson stopped in one of the middle of his talks and said, "I've got it. I've got it now! I'm sorry. Everything I've been saying up to this point is wrong. But I can explain why."

Bruce Wilkinson's startling awakening caused everyone in attendance to get down on his knees and pray. The insight being given to the group was clearly not merely of Bruce Wilkinson's making. That was the moment, the time, the day, on which the *Fellowship of Companies for Christ* was truly born. It was the fellowship's Pentecost.

The secular understanding of business lies in return on investment. Business uses capital to produce profit, and the more profit the better. Making a profit is the sum and substance of a business's purpose. Most Christians essentially believed this too, as Wilkinson's audience readily admitted. The only difference, really, was that they thought a portion of these profits ought to be devoted to God. Wilkinson saw this as being totally wrong.

A Christian understanding of business, Wilkinson realized, lay in the priesthood of all believers. As a priest every Christian offers back to God the gifts of God, praising God even as he uses these gifts for God's purposes. That's not something that only a clergyman does full-time. That's everyone's full-time job. It's humanity's basic purpose. These acts of giving back—of sacrifice—multiply God's gifts, just as Jesus multiplied five loaves and two fishes to feed the five thousand, just as the good stewards from Jesus's parables multiply the talents with which they are entrusted. Only by "giving one's company to Christ" can a believer realize a business's true potential, because the business's purposes are God's purposes. And God is in the business of redeeming the whole world and making it perfect and new again. Our own businesses can and should be part of His.

Both the secular and Christian understandings of business see human enterprise as a multiplier of resources, a creator of wealth. The bottom line for a Christian business is obedience to the will of God. Its wealth creation has not only a temporal dimension but an eternal one as well. Its profits are not ends in themselves but serve greater ends.

Wilkinson counseled that this did not mean Christian business owners should neglect making a profit. He warned against a false spirituality that would lead the owner to presume that if he had spiritual purposes in mind then God would take care of practical matters. No, one had "to work one's own vineyard." Sheer labor would always be required.

He also taught, wisely, that running a business for Christ did not simplify operations but added a new set of obligations and responsibilities.

How could one know what these were? As always in the life of faith, there were two dimensions: the broad principles of God's will are readily known through the Scriptures; how these principles open up possibilities cannot be known in advance. Trust comes into play step by step. This is challenging, to say the least, especially to business owners whose job is often to mitigate risk even in the midst of new ventures. The risk of the Christian life cannot be mitigated. From the human side it appears total. Because the will of God proceeds from an utterly trustworthy source, however, the risk is only apparent rather than real. Still, "to walk by faith, not by sight" remains a continual struggle.

Nevertheless, business owners can know the essential priorities of their "priesthoods" and the most immediate ways these translate into business terms. Wilkinson put forward four essential motions in what he described as the looping process of Christian growth, one in which every rising challenge brought God's answer as a call to obedience that, if followed, presented in time another challenge.

As God's priests, he said, our first obligation is to attend to our own walk with God. Because what God asks of us can often be counterintuitive, we must ground ourselves in the knowledge and love of God. Only in this way can we respond to God's call and have the courage necessary to take action on the basis of faith.

As priests, our businesses are our platforms—one might say altars—for accomplishing God's purposes. His first purpose is to call everyone to a saving knowledge of Jesus Christ. The Christian business owner must be concerned for the salvation of his employees, for his clients, for his vendors, for his community, and for those beyond his community in an ever-widening circle. Wilkinson pointed out that beginning with one's employees and those closest to home follows the inherent pattern of the Great Commission: "But you will receive power when the Holy Spirit comes on you; and you will be my witnesses in Jerusalem, and in all Judea and Samaria, and to the ends of the earth" (Acts 1:8). For the business owner, his "Jerusalem" is his business—the center of his world. He is often persuaded to go "to the ends of the earth" first, but while that's important, it's the last step in his priestly ministry. Being persuaded that it's the first is a distortion.

Business owners need to be concerned for the sanctification of their employees and others touched by their businesses. Wilkinson advised keeping a closet full of helpful books about marriage, drug addiction, and other common troubles. He urged his listeners to put on marriage and child-rearing seminars for their employees at company expense. People confronting life's problems are ready to listen to God's solutions.

Finally, a measure of one's profits, as well as one's own personal income, ought always to be reserved for service to one's employees, the community, and a selection of Christian ministries. Again, the emphasis needed to be on those closest to hand first.

The new fellowship's abiding question, "What would Jesus do?" now had the tenets of an enduring answer.

When Jimmy Pursell stood to give his testimony at the first meeting of what would become the Fellowship of Companies for Christ, Wilkinson's teaching about what it meant to run a company for Christ lay months in the future. These would appear to be prescriptive—a guide to Christian business. They were really *descriptive*, the discovery or re-discovery of biblical revelation. The consistency of God's character can be seen both in biblical revelation and in what God calls faithful people to do. Reflecting on what Jimmy said that day at the Marriott Motor Lodge, he had already incorporated Wilkinson's four priorities into the way he did business. He was deepening his faith and changing personal habits in order to be a more effective witness. He had hired John Riley to bring the messages of salvation and sanctification to his employees. He had already set up a fellowship among his town's business leaders that quickly attracted 90 percent or more of the town's leadership. Riley also spoke to this fellowship as well as to an ever-widening circle of groups across the American southeast. Jimmy was proceeding exactly as prescribed: "from Jerusalem to Judea to Samaria to the ends of the earth."

At this point Jimmy had no idea how his influence might extend to the ends of the earth. That lay in the future and in the unknown, mysterious aspect of God's will. Its accomplishment would be slow and methodical in coming, but in retrospect so shocking as to bear the marks of the miraculous.

The adventure of Jimmy's life had only begun. It started with his obedience to a calling he hardly understood. It gained tremendously from the perspective offered by the Fellowship of Companies for Christ.

This organization has gone on to influence thousands of businesses around the world. It has been in the forefront of the "business as mission" movement that is now, at last, at the cutting edge of the mission movement around the world.

In addition to Bobby and Bert, the original board consisted of five additional founders: Larry Burkett, Thomas Harris, Bill Leonard, Jim Moye, and Ben Lively. They quickly asked Jimmy and Smith Lanier to join them.

This board would serve intact throughout the 1980s and 1990s. For a long time the board thought the fellowship could not fund an international effort. They were welcoming and gave counsel to such visitors as Ken Crowell, who went on to found Galtronics in Israel, which won the Kaplan Award as one of the nation's best companies and was proclaimed a blessing to Israel on the front page of the *Jerusalem Post*. They also influenced Cade Willis, who moved his family to Singapore, took on ten unreached people groups to evangelize, and became a senior Christian statesman of that globally important city-state.

Such experiences gradually convinced the board to think bigger. In 1990, the Fellowship of Companies for Christ decided that a group started by "a bunch of Southern white boys" might have relevance internationally. The name became the Fellowship of Companies for Christ International, and the principals began to take mission trips to understand how the Fellowship might help in other parts of the world. This was fueled by a pivotal conference in 1996 that raised $2.5 million dollars. The recession of 2008 hurt, but the Fellowship has a vital presence in India, Singapore, Malaysia, and the Philippines.

This was a start, but only a start, to Jimmy's witness reaching the ends of the earth.

Jimmy and his older sister Dot, Talladega, Alabama, 1933.

Jimmy (#75 running back) and the Talladega High School football team, 1946.
The Talladega team only lost one game in 1947 against the Sylacauga Aggies, a game in which Jimmy broke his leg. Ironically, while in the hospital, Jimmy met Sylacauga native Jim Nabors, they became lifelong friends, and through Jim Nabors Jimmy met Chris Parker – the rest is history.

Jimmy attending a family reunion in 1947.
Jimmy is standing by his mother, Eunice. His father, Howard, is seated with a pipe.

Jimmy, an aviation cadet, stationed at Mather Air Force Base in Sacramento, California, 1952.

Wedding of Jimmy Pursell and Chris Parker, July 10, 1953.
Also shown are Chris Parker's parents, Ola and Howard Parker Sr., and Chris's younger brother, Howard Jr. Jim Nabors sang, ushered, and served as best man – preceding his notoriety as an entertainer. The ceremony was held at Mather Air Force Base.

Jimmy and Chris Pursell exiting the chapel as newlyweds.

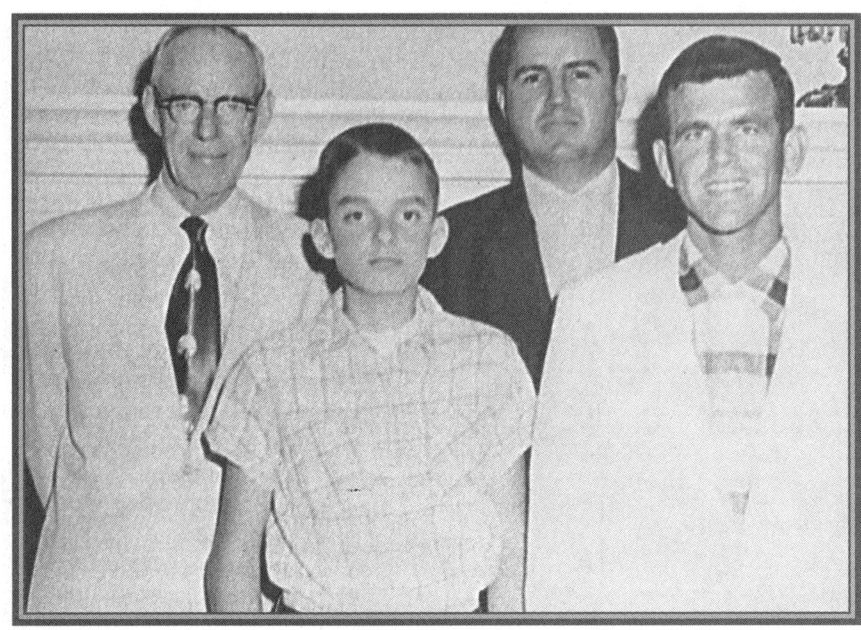

Father-in-law and employer Howard Parker Sr., Howard Jr., Bill Nichols, and Jimmy attending a fertilizer convention at the Greenbrier Hotel in West Virgina, 1958. Jimmy began employment as a salesman with the Parker Fertilizer Company in 1956.

Jimmy, Howard Parker Sr., and Howard Parker Jr., Dupont office, Atlanta, Georgia, 1961. At this time Jimmy was in his early 30s. He and Chris had three children, Taylor, Chris, and David.

Jimmy receiving the coveted Slater-Wright Award at the Southern Nurseryman's Association annual convention, Atlanta, 1976. This annual award was presented to the person who was voted as the top contributor to the nursery industry.

Jimmy, one of the keynote speakers for the inaugural gathering of the Fellowship of Companies for Christ International (FCCI), 1980. Jimmy served on the board of the FCCI, also helping to fund the organization. FCCI has grown to be a worldwide organization of Christian business owners aspiring to use their businesses as a platform – sharing the gospel of Jesus Christ.

Jimmy standing by controlled-release fertilizer samples – later building an SCU plant in Sylacauga, Alabama, 1986. These early samples (Sulfur Coated Urea) were produced by the Tennessee Valley Authority in Muscle Shoals, Alabama. As a pioneer in this industry, Jimmy proceeded to build the SCU facility in Sylacauga.

Jimmy and friend Bert Stumberg, South Korea. Jimmy had been destined to serve in the Korean conflict in the early 1950s, but the war came to an end before he was called to duty. He visited the battlefields in which he never had to fight. Jimmy and Bert served together on FCCI's board of directors and remained close friends.

Jimmy with a bag of Sta-Green Nursery fertilizer – one of the many successful products he launched over his fifty-year career in the fertilizer business.

Jimmy welcoming over 700 guests at the opening of FarmLinks Golf Club, Pursell Farms, June 2003. In attendance were local and industry friends, family, the governor of Alabama Bob Riley, now famous Jim Nabors, Miss America Nicole Johnson, and many golf course industry CEOs. Jimmy's grand-daughters Peggy, Vaughan, Chrissy, and Ramsey Pursell sang at the event.

Jimmy and sons David and Taylor enjoy a friendly game of golf.

Jimmy and Auburn's Heisman Trophy-winning running back Bo Jackson.

The immediate family of Jimmy and Chris Pursell – Taylor, Chris (Fleming), and David. Not shown are ten grandchildren and (now) five great-grandchildren.

Jimmy and Chris with "Aubie," the official mascot of Auburn University. Grandson Martin Pursell served two years in Auburn's Aubie program. Aubie has won eight national mascot championships over the years, including 2014.

Jimmy and Chris with childhood friend Jim Nabors, celebrating Nabors' seventieth birthday.

Left to right, Chris Pursell, her sister Julia Oliver, Jimmy's sister Dot Power, and Jimmy.

Receiving the annual Lifetime Achievement Award by Auburn University College of Human Sciences, in New York City at the United Nations Building, in December 2012. Shown left to right, Bill Hardgrave, dean of the Harbert College of Business; June Henton, dean of the College of Human Sciences; Chris and Jimmy Pursell; and Achilles Armenakis, Auburn University's James T. Pursell Sr. Eminent Scholar in Ethics and director of the Center of Ethical Organizational Cultures in the Harbert College of Business.

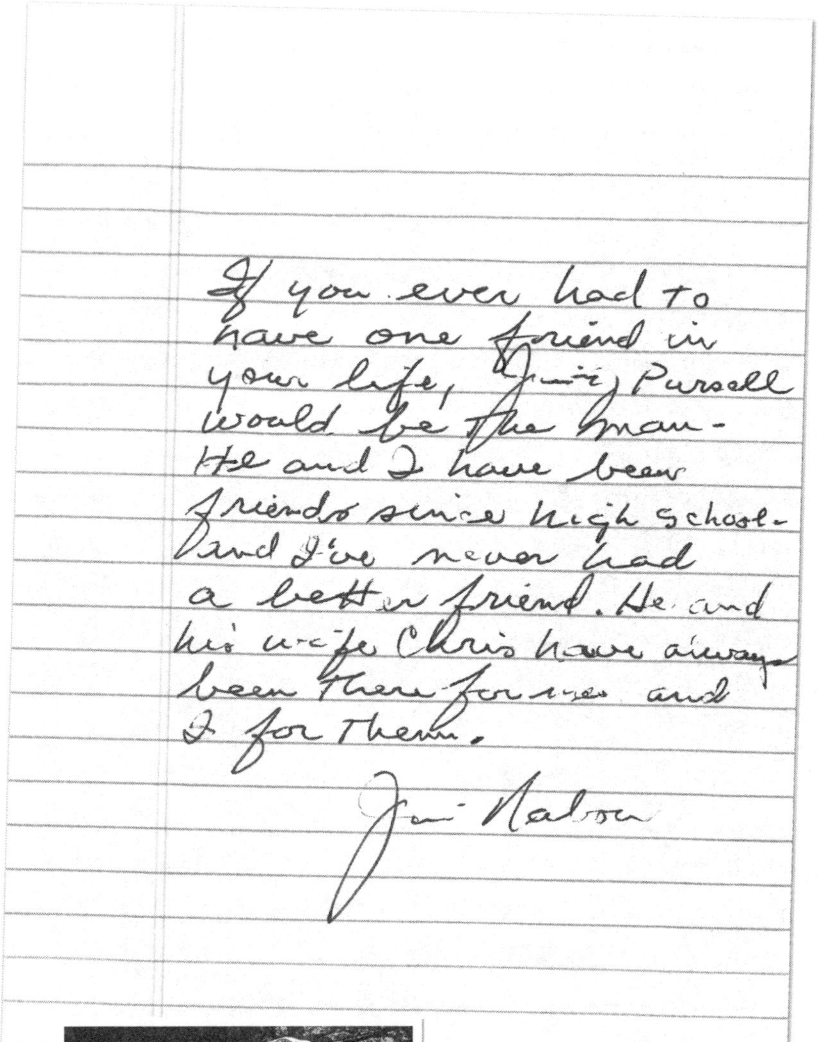

If you ever had to have one friend in your life, Jimmy Pursell would be the man. He and I have been friends since high school and I've never had a better friend. He and his wife Chris have always been there for me and I for them.

Jim Nabors

CHAPTER SEVEN

Business by the Numbers

In the summer of 1976, Jimmy and Chris's eldest son, Taylor Pursell, left Auburn University and joined the company. Taylor did not grow up assuming that he would one day run the family business, but from the age of twelve, when he began shoveling cottonseed, to his disastrous supervision of bone-meal packaging to the various jobs that had followed throughout his college summers, Taylor became increasingly interested in the company. He never truly considered doing anything other than joining the family business. Jimmy wanted it that way not only for Taylor but Chrissy and David as well. One of his principle goals in life was growing a business in which his children could earn their livelihoods, if they so desired.

The rest of the company's management did not feel as comfortable with Taylor's presence. In fact, they held a closed-door meeting in which they considered how they could keep Taylor as far away as possible. Opinionated, stubborn, and prone to wild expenditures (he once ordered a Datsun 240-Z sports car using the name he shared with his father—without the "Jr."), in the minds of Jimmy's leadership team, Taylor's obvious talents did not compensate for his callow judgment.

Mr. Parker had broken Jimmy in with a sales territory—a practice that Jimmy had followed with other young executives, including Taylor.

Perhaps as a result of the leadership team's desire to place Taylor "as far away as possible" from the home office, he was given a completely new market in which Parker Industries had no established accounts, the Carolinas. Taylor moved to Chapel Hill and, touring the countryside in a more humble company car than the Z, began opening up his territory to Parker Fertilizer's Sta-Green line. He did this by begging nurseries and lawn and garden shops for initial orders. These orders materialized only because Taylor promised to return on the weekends to sell the products personally to customers. Like his father, Taylor was an exceptionally good salesman.

No doubt Jimmy knew the machinations of his leadership team in regard to Taylor. He also knew his son and the potential of the Carolinas as a market. Sending Joseph into Egypt one more time might not work out as his leadership team supposed, Jimmy must have been thinking. Instead, what the leadership team had meant as an exile became, as in the original story, a means for good. During the next years, Parker Fertilizer's sales boomed. Sales had grown from around 2 million in 1965, when Jimmy was first fully in control of the company, to about 7 million in 1982. Much of this growth had occurred after Taylor joined the company and opened up the Carolinas. When Taylor returned to the home office after five years, having built up the business from scratch in the Carolinas, he returned with a legitimate claim to authority. Jimmy told all his children they had "to earn their wings," and each, in turn, would do so.

Chrissy graduated from Auburn in 1978 with a degree in special education. She came back to Sylacauga to teach, but Jimmy lured her away with a job offer after the first year. Like Jimmy and Taylor, Chrissy was given a sales territory as a first assignment—but much closer to home than Taylor, as she handled accounts in Alabama and Georgia. With a personality much like her father's and a network of girlfriends spread across Alabama, with whom she spent the nights while traveling, Chrissy took to the job immediately.

Although selling fertilizer remained a "man's world," the way had been prepared by her father, whom many of her customers knew personally. Diminutive in size, she worried about what people thought initially. "I'm sure I looked like I was twelve years old because I was so young and just five feet tall," she says. "I can't imagine what they were thinking when I walked through the door." She made an impression, nevertheless, and still runs into people to this day who remember her from that time. After two-and-a-half years traveling, she started a customer service department. The service department supported the salespeople, routed orders, and fielded customer calls. She would stay active in the business for the next six years.

The youngest of the children, David Pursell, married his college sweetheart, Ellen Shipman, in August of 1981. He had virtually completed his degree at Auburn and was ready to join the company.

He too started out in sales. David was naturally a dreamer and spent his childhood "in his own world." He loved drawing and could lose himself for hours sketching on copier paper. He went on to study commercial art in college and eventually became known for his pencil-portraits of well-known golfers that hang in many prestigious country clubs, including The Greenbrier, Shoal Creek, and Augusta National. David found sales more of a challenge than his siblings, although Jimmy often opened up the way by initiating accounts and handing them over to his son to develop. David soon hit his stride in the company, though, by starting an in-house advertising agency. He poured all of his creative talent into promoting the company's products.

Taylor, Chrissy, and David relish the memories of the 1980s, as they were at the company, working side by side with their father when he was at the height of his powers and making the crucial decisions that would finally turn a little family-owned company in Sylacauga, Alabama, into a national powerhouse.

On Christmas Day in 1983 a story in the *Birmingham News* appeared about the Auburn Technical Assistance Center (ATAC). Funded by a government grant, ATAC provided management and technical expertise to Alabama businesses. This public/private venture was run by Dr. Achilles Armenakis and patterned after the agricultural extension model, except that its clients were required to pay consulting fees. ATAC employed three professionals,

Armenakis and two management scientists, as well as three graduate students and a secretary. It was also able to call upon members of Auburn's many other departments and so could provide a wide range of expertise.

Armenakis grew up in his family's restaurant business in Louisiana, established after his family emigrated from Greece. Working in every job the restaurant business demanded, he helped pay his way through his bachelor's degree and an MBA. Once he completed a doctorate in business administration, he was invited to teach at Auburn and four years later was named director of ATAC. Jimmy saw that Armenakis's background in a family business prepared him to understand the challenges of Parker Fertilizer. Armenakis specialized in organizational change, and Parker Fertilizer was certainly changing (at times in ways that Jimmy felt threatened to go out of control).

The recent growth of the company had brought problems. Parker Fertilizer had established its own trucking division to deliver its more than three hundred products, but Jimmy had done some investigating and found that the company could save $250,000 per year in costs if it outsourced transportation. Outsourcing might be best for the bottom line, but Jimmy worried what would happen to his employees in the trucking division and their families. Many had been with the company for years.

He wondered if the problem might take care of itself through growth, which was another debate in the company. Taylor looked forward to doing "90 million by 1990," but other managers were resisting his preference for an aggressive growth plan. Personally, Jimmy favored adopting an aggressive approach, but he also heard the complaints from his salespeople that they couldn't work longer hours and were already traveling more than they expected.

Most disturbing of all, the profitability of the company was not increasing as it should have in proportion to sales. The top line had nearly tripled, which meant that the bottom line should have multiplied exponentially through economies of scale. That had not happened. Parker Fertilizer's sales were increasing, but the profit margin was volatile and depended, in large part, on a single private-label contract.

In the prime of life he worked tirelessly on the business. His bent was to sell and market, but he paid attention to every other aspect of the business to the extent possible. In 1970 he had detected inconsistencies in the orders, the bills of lading, and the sell-through volume. He hired the Pinkerton Detective Agency to place agents as new workers throughout Parker Fertilizer's transportation division.

He found out that most of his truck drivers serving the Atlanta area were involved in a theft scheme by short-loading Pursell's customers. The drivers would load up the trucks for their night delivery shift, between three to five tons per load, and drive until they reached the lumberyard in Tallapoosa, Alabama. Arriving just before the break of daylight, the trucks would pull in, mount the scales and honk their horns, notifying the owner of their arrival. The owner would then direct the driver where to unload the "loot," and after doing so, pay the driver off in cash in order to cover up the transaction. Their entire process only took five minutes to perform.

After receiving a call about the potential scandal, Jimmy and his brother-in-law, Ken Power, decided to investigate further by involving both the Alabama and Georgia's Bureaus of Investigation. Once everything was in place, Pursell's detective was sent as a truck driver into Tallapoosa lumberyard in hopes of catching the owner red-handed. The plan went off perfectly. After the practiced signal from the truck driver was given—meaning money had been exchanged—the investigators moved in and placed the owner under arrest.

The ringleaders were fired. Jimmy showed mercy, however, to long-time employees whose involvement was minimal. They were disciplined but retained.

Still, by Christmas Day of 1983, Jimmy felt he was "losing control of his company." He called Dr. Achilles Armenakis the next day. He asked Armenakis to come to Sylacauga for a visit. He would give him a tour of the plant, introduce him to the company's key managers, and then discuss a consulting arrangement.

Armenakis brought with him one of his colleagues, Henry Burdg. Henry's father had worked for a family-owned steel plant in Cleveland, where Henry also worked in the summers. Fascinated by flying, Henry took his bachelor's degree in aviation management and then worked for two years with an airport engineering consulting firm for two years. Then he earned an MBA and was subsequently hired by ATAC. Armenakis thought Henry's familiarity with manufacturing and engineering processes might be a particular help if Mr. Pursell chose to hire them.

When Armenakis and Burdg arrived on the designated morning, Jimmy gave them a tour of the plant, showing them the mixing and packaging processes. For a manufacturer, these processes were fairly simple, although technical problems came up, like controlling the plant's humidity. Armenakis and Burdg had worked with many types of companies, including a foundry; however, they did not have any particular expertise in fertilizer, as Armenakis readily confessed. Jimmy thought that wouldn't be an impediment, as managing, in Jimmy's view, was a fairly generic process. Managing a fertilizer mixer is much like managing a foundry.

Not many steps into the plant, Armenakis saw a box in a corner that was being dripped on through a leak in the roof. He asked what was in it. The plant manager who had joined them explained that it was something called a "personal computer." No one knew how to use it yet, so they were just keeping it there for now. Armenakis made a mental note.

After the tour, Jimmy expressed his concerns to Armenakis and Burdg. Jimmy said he wanted to retire in about fifteen years, when he planned on turning over the company's management to his two sons and daughter. He wanted to make sure he handed over a thriving business. He needed to know whether Parker Fertilizer should attempt to expand, and if so, how fast. Jimmy, like his eldest son, favored an aggressive growth strategy, but he wanted to make sure the company could execute such a strategy.

Armenakis and Burdg explained that they could facilitate this process. What Jimmy had described demanded organizational change—their specialty—but Jimmy needed to understand that it would demand that Jimmy, his managers, and their staff would have to start doing things differently—a lot differently. The company had to prepare itself for growth before a strategy could be planned and executed.

Jimmy said, "I feel your experience is important to working with us. Why don't we go back to the office to continue this discussion with the other managers?"

At the meeting, Armenakis explained that the purpose of their work with the company would be to determine the company's requirements in order to develop and implement an aggressive growth strategy. That let loose the underlying tensions. The complaints about long hours and traveling days emerged. How could a new growth strategy be implemented when everyone was already working as hard as they could? The managers bickered about whether they should be putting more energy into local markets. A sales manager pointed out that one of their largest accounts was in New Jersey. A distribution manager objected that they were too far away.

"What did that have to do with anything?" the sales manager asked.

"Freight charges!" came the quick reply.

Armenakis pointed out that the project would involve two phases. First, a diagnostic evaluation as to how the company operated benchmarked against best practices. The second phase would depend on what the diagnostics revealed. Armenakis and Burdg would present what the diagnostics revealed to the group and then help them arrive at a decision as to what needed to be done.

The comptroller of the company, Bill McDowell, wanted to know, from Jimmy, if he truly felt this was necessary. He had been through similar reviews in the past and found them to be time-consuming.

"I realize it will be," Jimmy said. "But I would like us to agree that we will make the time. It is the only way we are going to map out our future."

After Jimmy gave this positive signal, his managers began reconciling themselves to the idea, and the meeting ended with the managers expressing their willingness to cooperate. One even volunteered that such a project should have been done a long time ago.

The manager meeting ended, Armenakis and Burdg met a final time with Jimmy before departing. As they talked, Armenakis noticed the plaque from the Fellowship of Companies for Christ beyond Jimmy's left ear on the wall. He did not know what this signified, although it gave him the feeling that this consulting job would result in an experience like no other.

Jimmy did worry aloud about losing control of the process and his company. That had been his underlying worry all along. What if Armenakis and Burdg only unleashed the demons of resentment and turf-guarding that was clearly present in the manager meeting?

Armenakis and Burdg had seen far worse in other introductory meetings. The managers' willingness to express their opinions was a good thing. What you really had to look out for was people keeping their own counsel and lying in the weeds, awaiting a chance to sabotage the process. Even in disagreement, the consultants sensed a fundamental solidarity among the managers. They assured Jimmy that the steps taken would help him gain more control, not lose it. They promised to send a follow-up proposal. Jimmy would see the results of their work privately at every stage before it was submitted to his leadership team, and the proposal would include circuit breakers if he decided to curtail the project.

Five weeks later, the work began. The company was small enough that a quantitative forced-answer instrument (choosing preferences on a one-to-five scale, for example) did not need to be developed. Rather, each manager would be interviewed over one hour and then, through recordings of the interviews and careful note-taking, the team's responses would be grouped in a systematic way by frequency and by what appeared to the consultants as underlying causal relationships.

Armenakis and Burdg asked simple and open-ended questions. They inquired about the company's strengths and its weaknesses.

Essentially what they found was that Parker Fertilizer had outgrown its "adaptive" mom-and-pop-style management techniques. In a mom-and-pop, everyone pitches in where needed. Titles, job descriptions, areas of responsibility, the authority to complete assigned responsibilities, the way in which compensation packages are rationalized—no one is too careful about these matters because the point is to be in business and *stay* in business. Anything that furthers the primary task of survival is welcomed, or at least accepted, without much resistance.

Parker Fertilizer had grown large enough that it needed to make the transition from its "adaptive"—or catch-as-catch-can—style of management to a planned style of management. That meant rationalizing—planning—how it operated from top to bottom. It needed to go from a mom-and-pop to a true corporate enterprise that embraced best practices across the board.

The leadership team had a fairly accurate understanding of how decisions were made, but no organizational chart existed. The company was divided into three separate corporate entities. Managers had responsibilities across these corporate entities, but in one of these branches, Manager A's authority could exceed Manager B's, and in another, Manager B's could exceed Manager A's—so people thought, at least. They weren't sure.

One of the frequent complaints that emerged from the interviews was that managers felt they did not have sufficient authority to carry out their assigned responsibilities, or they were unsure of how far their authority extended. This had many negative effects, effects that the consultants could see but to which the managers remained blind. Despite their protests about how hard everyone was working, managers used the confusion in authority as an excuse for poor work habits. They felt balked in carrying out their responsibilities, so they just threw up their hands and let things go. In the interviews, team members admitted that they had tried to have strategic meetings in the past, but, unable to reach a consensus, these had been abandoned.

The confusion in lines of authority created by the three separate entities also manifested itself in accounting practices, as all three entities shared one balance sheet.

When Armenakis and Burdg delivered their preliminary diagnostic report to Jimmy, it contained a lot of bad news. The company needed to know more clearly what it was about. A mission statement needed to be written; the aforementioned organization chart devised, with appropriate adjustments in responsibilities; a job description written for each employee; and compensation packages—another chief cause of resentment—needed benchmarked against the levels of compensation in other companies with due adjustments for cost of living. In particular, merit pay or bonuses needed rationalizing; there had to be a reliable measure about the added value those rewarded were bringing to the company. Yearly reviews of each employee's job performance needed to be instituted.

The worst news of all was that the company was essentially flying blind when it came to running its manufacturing operation. This addressed the stubborn profitability problem and divided into two aspects, both of which pointed back to data collection and, ultimately, accounting practices.

The three manufacturing plants were run on the basis of maximizing output. The largest orders took precedence without regard to the margins on these products. The company could actually be more profitable, as Armenakis and Burdg discovered, if it ran its manufacturing plants at lower capacity but gave precedence to products with higher margins. No one knew about this because the company lacked the means to run scenarios as to the priority assigned to one product or mix of products versus another.

Accounting was still being performed via hand-ledger. That sounds impossibly outdated now, but in the winter of 1984, the American business world was still two quarters away from Apple's ground-breaking "1984" ad that debuted at that summer's Olympics. IBM had introduced the personal computer only three years before, in 1981. The digital revolution was still in its infancy, with Parker Fertilizer's first machine sitting in its box under a leaky roof.

Armenakis and Burdg noted in particular that the costing system of sales was seriously askew. All transportation costs were assigned to one line item in the expense section of the profit-and-loss statement, as if the cost of delivering a truckload to New Jersey was the same, per unit, as it was to Birmingham. Armenakis remembers well the follow-up session in which the leadership team realized that its golden, $1 million contract in New Jersey, nearly 15 percent of the company's total revenues, was actually fool's gold, as it was draining profits out of the business. The distribution manager's worries about freight charges proved all too true. Mr. Pursell and a sales manager were soon on a plane to New Jersey to try to keep the customer at a price Parker Fertilizer could actually afford. In the end, the contract was cancelled, but with the happy result that Parker Fertilizer's profitability increased!

The findings of Armenakis and Burdg's diagnostics would have been hard to hear for any CEO who, like Jimmy, had been working sixty hours a week for years to ensure the proper functioning of his company. It's not easy to hear that people you have been paying well for years are resentful and use impediments to problem-solving as an excuse to do nothing. A smart man and a keen observer of human behavior, however, Jimmy knew such problems existed already, if he could not quite figure out how to solve them alone. He was humble enough to accept the findings of Armenakis and Burdg without any defensiveness, immediately expressing his gratitude for the work accomplished.

Parker Fertilizer was more ready for changes in the organization than the problems might have indicated because of one paramount factor: Jimmy had credibility among his employees. In subsequent scholarly work, Armenakis found that a leader's credibility consists in four attributes: (1) honesty, (2) competence, (3) inspiration, and (4) vision. Organizational change depends on related factors as well, but it can only begin at the top. "Revolutions from below," for all their present hype, do not produce the kinds of lasting changes that become institutionalized.

No one had forgotten the day in 1976 when Jimmy announced he was dedicating his company to Christ. Nor did they fail to observe how he had consistently followed through on this commitment, taking risks in doing so. He had always treated people honestly, and he insisted on his employees doing the same, as evidenced by the Pinkerton episode of 1970.

As far as competence went, he was clearly the firm's chief rainmaker and thoroughly understood every part of the operation. No one could see him strike up friendship after friendship with potential clients without being inspired. In 1986, his vision had been responsible for the company's move into sulfur-coated urea time-release products, which had differentiated Parker Fertilizer from its competitors and made way for the company's recent growth. Jimmy was credible.

The management reforms that were recommended by Armenakis and Burdg, particularly as they applied to human resource issues, are by now in almost equal measure standard practice and too often conveniently ignored by management. How many employees have received an excellent yearly review and been fired two months later? Most have lived through corporate consultation processes that are transparently political cover for what management wants to do anyway.

Happily, this was not the case at Parker Fertilizer. Jimmy allowed the results of Armenakis and Burdg's diagnostics to be shared with all his managers, including those findings that made him look bad. The consultants offered that they could proceed in two ways: either coming up with their own recommendations that management could then implement as it chose or moderating discussions among the leadership as they found their own path. The team quickly chose the latter. They wanted to be helped, not told.

Every Tuesday over the coming weeks, Armenakis and Burdg drove early in the morning from Auburn to Sylacauga. Each working session was scheduled for three hours, between 8:30 a.m. and 11:30 a.m. Jimmy or someone else began each with a prayer and ended each with a prayer. These were true working sessions and sometimes extended far beyond the scheduled time, which saw Armenakis and Burdg heading back to Auburn in the dark. Gradually, issues pertaining to lines of authority and areas of responsibility were sorted out. The team formulated the purpose and goals of the company. A corporate divisional organization chart and detailed divisional organization chart were constructed. A detailed operational plan was adopted that encompassed five projects: job descriptions, a training program, performance reviews, development of information systems, and a strategic marketing plan. The leaders of these projects were established and a timeline adopted for their completion.

The best thing to come out of this consultation project addressed the worst finding in the diagnostic phase. The company simply could not develop the data it needed to run its manufacturing and other operations in the most profitable way. Everyone saw the need to hire a director of management information systems.

The new hire turned out to be Arnold Cleghorn, a strapping man with a rumbling bass voice, a John Henry of pile-driving legend, who had the brilliant mind of the age's emerging hero: the nerd. Arnold Cleghorn started out, like Jimmy Pursell's father, as a teacher; in Arnold's case, a math teacher. Also like Jimmy's father, he soon figured out that he could never make an adequate living in the public schools of Alabama. So he sat himself down and learned how to program computers from a manual—all by himself, with no assistance whatsoever.

During one of the work sessions, Armenakis and Burdg gave the leadership team a three-day seminar in the use of VisiCalc, an early spreadsheet program. VisiCalc was rudimentary and could only handle data in a 64-cell by 64-cell spreadsheet. Today, comparable programs expand almost infinitely. Even so, the seminar on VisiCalc had the revolutionary impact on Parker Fertilizer that spreadsheet programs were having in virtually every American business sector at the time. Managers saw how they could run scenarios comparing the profitability of one manufacturing sequence against another, and they could do so virtually in realtime as orders came in. Since Parker Fertilizer's manufacturing process consisted of mixing commodities it received from elsewhere, the new program could also be used to track shipments and supplies in hand and match these with proposed manufacturing scenarios.

Arnold Cleghorn soon delivered to the company an information technology tool that may not even have had a name at that point. Now we know it as an intranet. He put an Apple computer on every desk and networked them all with a mini-computer, using it, as we would now say, as a server. The managers in charge of the company's various operations could now trade information and collaborate in decision making immediately, without ever leaving their desks. Work output soared.

Cleghorn's expertise supplied another invaluable tool: risk assessment. He was the guy who could run and crunch the numbers. He became Jimmy's invaluable backstop because he could determine so accurately what any new initiative might cost and whether the company could afford it. His facility with data brought a new type of confidence to the firm.

Even as Armenakis and Burdg helped the company prepare for an aggressive growth strategy, Jimmy Pursell pursued a fundamental change in the company's approach to manufacturing that would be the principle means of future growth. Jimmy's understanding of the digital revolution to come may have been limited, but he grasped absolutely how technological innovation could differentiate a company's products and increase its profitability many times over. He had been hampered by his inability to build a Sulfur Coated Urea (SCU) plant in 1986, once the technology was given by the TVA to private industry. The scale of the project would have overwhelmed Pursell Industries if the company had taken it on alone. He made several attempts to build such a plant, but the partnership arrangements he tried to put together failed to materialize.

Still, Jimmy remained undeterred in seeking technological breakthroughs. He wanted the company to become a "basic" manufacturer of their products. As he said to Achilles Armenakis, Parker Fertilizer was only a "mixer" at the time. They imported train carloads of basic materials and then mixed them together, packaged the mixtures, and sold them under their brand names, Sta-Green and others. With the advent of sulfur-coated urea products, the mixing became less important. Mostly they simply rebranded a ready-made product that came from other suppliers.

Jimmy thought there might be another and better way to deliver a time-release fertilizer other than supplying a sulfur coating. One of the company's consultants, Ray Shirley, had experience with manufacturing. He appointed Ray the head of a small research and development team.

Ray thought they might use a natural material as the casing for the fertilizer granules. The substance to be used would have to be light and degrade slowly.

Ray Shirley's choice? Popcorn.

The head of Research and Development purchased just about every hot-air popcorn popper in northern Alabama until he had more than three hundred in a portion of one warehouse devoted to his pilot project. He started popping. No one was supposed to know what he was doing, but the smell of popcorn wafted out from the warehouse night and day and could be detected for miles around.

Popcorn was an extremely lightweight delivery system—there was no doubt about that. Unfortunately, it attracted every rat in the surrounding county. They chewed holes in the packaging and gorged on a popcorn feast. What the rats didn't consume was then spoiled by moisture that came in through the rat holes. The popcorn gambit wasn't working, but it wasn't totally without promise either.

While popcorn proved a disastrous delivery system, Ray Shirley speculated that the machinery he had built could be used to produce the SCU product the TVA invented. Ray and his crew tried it. The drum they had constructed turned out to be capable of producing one ton of SCU fertilizer per day. They expanded what they had constructed and found they could produce several tons in an hour.

The scale of the project remained a problem. For a new SCU plant to be profitable, it needed to produce twenty-five thousand tons per year. Parker was only using five thousand at the time internally.

In a masterstroke, Jimmy solved this problem by entering into a pre-construction agreement with Vigoro for twelve thousand tons per year. His company retained total control and ownership of the plant, but their risk was hedged—in fact, virtually eliminated—by knowing that they would sell nearly 70 percent of the plant's production before even breaking ground. In order to keep competitors from jumping the arrangement in some way, Pursell Industries and Vigoro kept the plant and their agreement absolutely secret. No grand announcements were made. Nothing was said until the plant was up and running.

Getting the plant up and running proved a last, anxiety-inducing hurdle. The day the plant was supposed to come online in 1985, the machinery failed to function. By then Chris and Jimmy were heavily involved in Christian ministries and were traveling through Asia on a philanthropic mission. They were in Canton, China, when they received the phone call that there was a problem. The new plant's machinery did not work. The staff at home did not know why.

Jimmy and Chris stayed up most of the night praying that the staff could get the plant working. They remember this night as the "prayer of Canton."

The next day, miraculously, the machinery turned over and SCU started rolling out by the ton.

The difference between being a basic manufacturer of a product and its reseller was like night and day in terms of profitability.

Jimmy and Chris could now think more seriously about how they might help the ministries they had come to see.

CHAPTER EIGHT

Explosive Growth

In the 1980s, as Jimmy began considering how to become a producer of sulfur-coated urea, he formed a second company, Pursell Industries, as the research-and-development arm of Parker Fertilizer. When the new sulfur-coated urea plant came online in 1985—only the fourth such plant built in the United States—it operated under the Pursell Industries banner. Ray Shirley and his team had finally worked out the engineering via the popcorn route. Jimmy's astute pre-sale of 40 percent of the plant's production mitigated the risk entailed; in fact, the plant was profitable from day one and its financing repaid within a year. Instead of being a reseller, Pursell Industries was now a basic producer of their product. Jimmy's dream of being able to customize solutions for various types of plants drew a huge step closer.

Not long after the plant's opening, Jimmy received a call from Lowe's. Lowe's proposed an on-site visit in order to talk about Pursell Industries supplying sulfur-coated urea. It wanted to fly seven representatives into Sylacauga on the corporation's plane. Jimmy invited the group to come see them in Alabama at their earliest convenience.

Nothing like this had ever happened before. The company had scratched and clawed its way into the marketplace by selling their product into the region's stores—and in Taylor's case, personally selling it out of the Carolinas' stores through personal demonstrations on Saturday mornings. They went to the customers; the customers never came to them. Not until now. How would they pull this off? The plant wasn't a showcase. In fact, it needed a good deal of cleaning up to be presentable.

The company did have a long history of Southern hospitality, though, notably at the Southern Nursery Men's Association. How might they be as welcoming to the Lowe's representatives? Not in Atlanta or at another convention center, but in Sylacauga?

Fortunately, love for the Alabama countryside ran deep within the family and the Pursells were in possession of some of the most picturesque land Alabama has to offer. Jimmy and Chris owned property that had once been cotton fields and timberland that they turned into a cattle ranch and dubbed Pennywinkle Farms.

The family's land acquisition had actually begun with Taylor. As a nineteen-year-old, Taylor bought a decaying Civil War–era mansion on twenty-five acres of land in nearby Fayetteville—the nucleus of what became Pennywinkle Farms. Moses Hamilton had built the place in 1852. The property sheltered close beside Chalybeate Mountain. Taylor's ambitions for the old house soon outstripped his financial resources.

The mansion had not been inhabited for years when Taylor bought it, and its large sitting rooms and bedrooms were being used to store hay and shelter animals—many of which were uninvited guests. Jimmy and Chris saw the potential of what Taylor had acquired, took over ownership, and made the house's restoration a family project. The house boasted thirteen-foot ceilings above plank wood floors. Five brick chimneys still in excellent condition buttressed its sides, and its framing consisted of solid, hand-hewn, white pine wood.

So the Pursells escorted the animals out, shoveled out the hay, accumulated dirt and broken wood lathing, and replastered virtually the entire house. They added new steps up to a wide front porch, which led through double-folding doors to a twelve-foot-wide dogtrot hallway. They refurbished the house with antiques and moved there on Thanksgiving Day 1978. Within ten years the Old Hamilton Place on Marble Valley Road found its way onto the Department of the Interior's National Register of Historical Places.

When Chrissy Pursell married Aaron Fleming in 1985, their wedding party gathered on the white-gravel driveway out front while the ceremony took place on the porch. The Old Hamilton Place also served as the venue for company Easter egg hunts, fishing "rodeos," and other company outings. Jimmy and Chris enjoyed having people out to the farm and decided to build a guesthouse next door to the main house. They built an Alabama "cabin" in a style that perfectly matched the Old Hamilton Place, slept six comfortably, and included a home office for Jimmy.

As it happened, then, the Pursells were more ready than they realized at first to host the visiting party from Lowe's. They went into overdrive preparing, nevertheless. They cleaned up the plant and put everyone in new uniforms.

Taylor had a particular hand in preparing twenty-four hours of Southern hospitality at its finest. When the Lowe's plane landed at the Sylacauga airport, the party was met by the high school marching band playing up a brassy storm. A police-escorted motorcade led into town and a visit to the plant. Then the executives were whisked out to Pennywinkle Farms, where the guests were billeted in the newly built guesthouse. For supper, there was a cookout at the Old Hamilton Place.

The team from Lowe's and the Pursell Industries team quickly came to know one another in this friendliest of settings. As the magic hour came on, the air became pure and sweet, and Chalybeate Mountain emblazoned the horizon in the last moments before evening with the resplendent reds and yellows of fall. Lively conversation and the telling of stories continued on into the night until, superbly fed and entertained, the visiting executives went off to their comfortable beds and a night of deep, restful sleep.

In the morning, the visiting executives and the Pursell Industries team had breakfast, discussing logistics and ways the two companies could enhance each other's businesses. Then, with handshakes and well wishes, the visitors were off again to the airport and gone.

Jimmy heard nothing for the first few days after the party departed and debated whether to call or leave the other company for the time being to its own counsel. Finally, a week later, another phone call. Lowe's wanted to switch all of its plants over from their current supplier of SCU to Pursell Industries. Their order constituted 40 percent of the new plant's capacity.

The Lowe's visit made a deep impression on everyone at Pursell Industries. For Jimmy it represented confirmation that the move to being a basic supplier would effect the transformation he had envisioned. His company might be located in a small-town setting, but Pursell Industries was now a national company. The one-time, fifty-mile radius of Sylacauga Fertilizer with its mixing, ginning, and warehousing operations had now rippled all the way out to the Atlantic. The largest potato-growing operation in the West, Simplot, which supplied all of the potatoes for McDonald's french fries, soon became an SCU customer and an eventual joint-venture partner. Harrell's Fertilizer, which eventually dominated the market east of the Mississippi, also came on board as a joint-venture partner. The revolution taking place in international shipping, which did so much to globalize agriculture, extended Pursell Industries' presence around the world.

Although Taylor prepared the schedule of the Lowe's visit, David Pursell would prove the most deeply affected by the experience. In the years ahead he would think long and hard about the power of having customers visit the company. It gave what would become Pursell Technologies the chance to provide simple education about their products in a friendly environment. It gave them the advantage of "home turf," where they could form good relationships in favorable circumstances. But the Lowe's people were unusual in wanting to come to Sylacauga. How could they get other customers to do they same? How could they provide a compelling reason to visit rural Alabama? David's answers to these questions would frame a future chapter in the company's history.

Jimmy Pursell believed that two major aspects of Pursell Industries' operations could still be improved. The idea of using popcorn as a delivery mechanism, even if it did not work, had at least a theoretical advantage that remained attractive. Pursell Industries had found a way to manufacture SCU fertilizers, but the company still had to license the technology from the TVA. It did not own this technological innovation and would always remain only one of several SCU suppliers. Jimmy, naturally, wanted a product he could patent, if that was possible.

Also, SCU fertilizers, although far superior to simple nitrogen-based mixes, could not be engineered to serve the different growth cycles of different plants. That was the ultimate solution—a truly customized solution for every plant imaginable, timed exactly to its growth cycle. The kernel of an SCU fertilizer burst immediately once penetrated by moisture, releasing all its nutrients. As a granular product, it could be distributed more evenly than a nitrogen mix, and the sulfur-coated granules of an application broke down one by one over a period of days. Still, the period over which the fertilizer was effective depended mostly on the amount of fertilizer distributed and the amount of moisture supplied. There was no way to time the release of the fertilizer to a plant's growth cycle. In this sense, SCU was like common fertilizer mixes: a one-size-fits-all solution.

His company transformed by technological innovation, Jimmy Pursell kept a sharp eye out for new approaches with promise. Through a trade journal, Jimmy learned of a man named John Detrick at Melamine Chemicals who was developing a polymer—or plastic—coating for fertilizer granules. Detrick called the process Reactive Layer Coating Urea (RLCU) because the polymers were actually made as the granules were coated. This introduced the possibility that the thickness of the coating could be varied virtually infinitely to very exact tolerances. The polymer coating of each granule would not break down all at once—like a sulfur-coated granule—but gradually release over a highly predictable amount of time determined by the coating's thickness. That meant, at least theoretically, that a fertilizer could be made to match the growth cycle of camellias and another fertilizer made for azaleas and another for bougainvillea and, in fact, a specific fertilizer for every plant in God's garden. Melamine Chemical Company received their first patents for this technology in 1987, but it was a long way, at that point, from being perfected.

It might never be perfected—or that was the judgment of Melamine Chemical. The company did not seem to understand the potential of Reactive Layer Coating (RLC) technology. At the time, they were more concerned with the ability to pay their employees an annual bonus. With the invaluable assistance of Arnold Cleghorn, Jimmy took advantage of Melamine's desire for cash to buy the rights to develop, manufacture, and market RLC fertilizers. He also persuaded John Detrick to join Pursell Industries in 1988 and set him up in a research facility to perfect the process.

Finally, Jimmy bought the patents as well, creating another corporation specifically for the purpose of holding these rights. In this way, even Pursell Technologies would have to pay a licensing fee to Jimmy's new independent company to exploit RLC. Jimmy hoped the new company would be a perpetual nest egg for his family.

Detrick was joined in his research-and-development work by Fred Carney. John Detrick produced small batches of experimental product, and Fred Carney tried to produce large machinery that could replicate John's improvements with the test batches. John was working on "bench scale" and Fred on a pilot plant scale. While John aimed to produce four or five pounds of the product, Fred tried to replicate his results at more than a thousand pounds an hour. For the pilot scale facility, Fred used Pursell Industries' no-longer-used truck shop adjacent to the lab.

Other members of the research-and-development team included a young engineer from India named Amit Roy. Twenty years later he would be asking potentially world-changing questions about whether fossil-fuel-based polymers might be replaced by biodegradable polymers.

In 1992, Parker Fertilizer Company became Pursell Industries. The name-change reflected the full engagement of Jimmy and his three children in the business and the company's transition to a basic supplier.

In 1991 and 1992, Pursell Industries felt confident enough in its RLC product to begin selling small quantities. The company did this mostly to obtain customer feedback. Customers reported problems. The first polymers used were essentially wax and melted at high temperatures. A better polymer formula fixed this problem.

These early problems did not keep Pursell Industries from making a big bet on RLC, as the company broke ground on a multimillion-dollar production facility in 1991. Nevertheless, even after the technical problems were solved, there remained a challenging marketing task.

RLC fertilizer cost more than other types. In the long run, it was more economical because it was more effective and required fewer applications. Potential customers needed to understand how it worked in order to overcome their price resistance. "Reactive Layer Coating" made immediate sense to few.

The eventual brand name, POLYON®, finally emerged through a contest David Pursell ran. In the end, John Detrick named his invention. "My idea for POLYON® came from a mix of thoughts," he reflected. "*Poly*mer coating *on* the granule, releases urea *on and on*. DuPont markets a polymer product with a well-recognized trade name, ny*lon*."

The look of the product also needed work. At first it was a brown color. Taylor did not like the idea of a brown product in Sta-Green fertilizers. He insisted, "We are going to grow *green* grass with a *green* controlled-release polymer-coated urea, not a brown one!"

Even after it had a great name and its distinctive green color, however, customers remained skeptical. POLYON®'s higher initial price demanded educating the customer as to its benefits. Fortunately, as a basic supplier, Pursell Industries no longer needed to hawk the product personally to end-users in lawn and garden stores as Taylor had done in the Carolinas. The customers who needed to understand POLYON® were now distributors, "formulators," who—as Parker Fertilizer had once done—repackaged the product under their own labels, horticulturalists of the major lawn and garden chains, and industrial users, particularly in the golfing industry.

The Lowe's experience came to mind. What could be better than having small parties of key people come to Sylacauga for tours of the plant and an educational presentation? They could show their guests the same Southern hospitality that had won over the Lowe's executives. And they could make it fun by including an outing—usually a trip to a golf course but on other occasions college football games and hunting excursions.

One of Pursell Industries' key people, Tim Orton, took the lead on this, arranging for party after party of six people (primarily golf course superintendents)—the number the guest house could accommodate easily—to come to Sylacauga. There was an informal rule that one of the people, a formulator or distributor, needed to be an enthusiastic supporter of POLYON®. Another had to have a measure of familiarity. That way the four who had never been exposed to the product before could verify what they were being told with peers.

The marketing tours followed a set schedule. Everyone would arrive at the Birmingham airport by 1 p.m., then go straight out to the golf course, and afterwards attend a fine dinner at a restaurant. Then the party was taken to the guesthouse to stay the night. In the morning, after an early jaunt for breakfast to Fayetteville's Kozy Korner or Sylacauga's Mama Ree's, the group would be given a tour of the POLYON® plant. POLYON® was an exceptionally clean product for a fertilizer, by virtue of its coating, so the tour defied visitors' expectations and lent credence to the high-tech nature of the product. Then everyone would sit down for an educational session with John Detrick, the "Father of POLYON®." Detrick was better in the lab than before a group, however, and Tim Orton was always there to translate Detrick's explanation of molecular biology into English. Detrick was given the nickname Mr. Wizard.

During the period when the tours took hold, from 1993 to 1997, Pursell Industries' relationships with two major customers, Simplot and Harrell's, became especially important. Jack Harrell made it mandatory for each of his salespeople to take two groups per year to Sylacauga. (Harrell's team of five salespeople eventually grew into more than ninety as they sold POLYON®.) Every new salesperson had to go through the "green needle," i.e., the Pursell tour. Simplot even formed a joint venture with Pursell called "Alida," a combination of the first letters of "Alabama" and "Idaho"—the bases of the two companies—to optimize their market position in the Western United States and in the Pacific Rim countries. The

Simplot connection also allowed Pursell Industries' products to penetrate throughout the western United States. The eventual joint venture with Harrell's was called "Florala," a combination of the first letters of Florida and Alabama. The market covered in the joint venture grew to be all states east of the Mississippi River.

With POLYON®, Jimmy realized his goals to become a basic manufacturer and to provide a customized product for every type of plant. Nothing else could yet match POLYON®'s benefits.

CHAPTER NINE
Ethics Is in His DNA

In 1992, the governor of Alabama, Guy Hunt, approached Jimmy Pursell about serving on the Alabama Ethics Commission. At the time, Governor Hunt was in serious trouble because of questions related to his own ethics.

Elected in 1986 and reelected in 1990, Guy Hunt was the first Republican governor in Alabama since Reconstruction. Democrats dominated other statewide offices, including the lieutenant governorship, held by Jim Folsom Jr., as well as the legislature. Hunt pressed forward with an agenda that included tort reform, which met with heavy opposition.

An autodidact who never went to college, Hunt was first elected to public office in 1964 as Cullman County's probate judge. In private life, he ran an egg farm, sold Amway products, and was an ordained Primitive Baptist minister. He represented a sea change in Alabama politics and naturally was watched closely by his opponents.

In 1991, as the result of a referral from the state's Ethics Commission, a grand jury was convened to consider charges brought against Governor Hunt. In the past three years, records showed that he had used state aircraft to preach at churches throughout the southeast and also for a ten-day vacation before a governor's conference in Seattle. At some of his preaching stops, he had received personal compensation. Hunt argued that a 1980 ruling by the Alabama Ethics Commission gave the governor broad powers to use state aircraft for personal reasons and that his security staff had advised him to keep the trips confidential. Nevertheless, the director of the state's Ethics Commission, Melvin Cooper, questioned whether the ruling applied to trips where a governor received personal compensation. Records revealed that as of August 1991 the governor's use of state aircraft on personal trips had cost the state \$184,000. Eventually, the state supreme court would rule that citizens had a right to sue the governor for reimbursement on those trips from which he had benefitted personally.

In this circumstance, Governor Hunt needed to nominate to the ethics board someone admired by all sides of the political spectrum. The board was and remains composed of five members, each of which serves a five-year term, with one new board member elected each year. The governor, the lieutenant governor, and the speaker of the house nominate members of the commission, and the state Senate must confirm these nominees.

Both Republicans and Democrats try to use the Ethics Commission as a political weapon. Every four years, or quadrennium, as they say in Alabama politics, when a new legislature is elected, the executive director of the Ethics Commission typically receives calls from new officeholders requesting leniency for a friend being investigated. The present director of the Ethics Commission, Jim Sumners, says he responds by telling the caller that he's welcome to call about the weather or sports scores or any topic at all other than an investigation. "We shouldn't be having this conversation," Sumner says, "and you should know that." Over the years the ethics board has acquired a sterling reputation for political independence, but that does not keep people from trying to manipulate it for their own ends.

Jimmy agreed to serve, his nomination and election went forward, and he began his work on the Ethics Commission September 1, 1992.

Just at the time that POLYON® was truly coming on the market, Jimmy somehow found the time to go through the five to six nearly book-length dossiers compiled on every case before the commission's monthly meeting.

The commission worked under guidelines that narrowed their focus and made their work so serious that the commission's executive director, Jim Sumner, compares a day's hearings to being beaten with a baseball bat. It takes a day or two to recover, he says. The commission has three charges: to investigate complaints against the now three hundred eight thousand state, county, and municipal workers; to render opinions as to one or more ethical standards when an opinion is specifically requested by a member of the legislature; and to register lobbyists and principals (those who employ lobbyists, individuals, businesses, and trade associations).

Investigations that went forward resulted in the five commissioners convening as a type of grand jury. Their deliberations were directed exclusively toward finding probable cause. When they found probable cause that the state's ethics law had been violated, their only recourse was to refer the matter for criminal prosecution to the state's attorney general or a district attorney. Minor filing offenses were misdemeanors, but abuse of office for personal gain was a Class B felony, punishable by up to twenty years in prison. About 85 percent of the cases that come before the commissioners are serious in nature, and the commissioners review few complaints that do not meet the probable cause standards.

The present director, Jim Sumners, says that his staff will not present a case where they do not believe probable cause exists and that ninety-seven out of one hundred cases presented are referred to the criminal justice system for prosecution. Of course, the staff deals with many complaints that prove dead ends, but the commissioners never see these. This was largely the case during Jimmy's time of service.

The people who are asked to serve as commissioners are, like Jimmy, those of standing within Alabama. They bring good judgment and a wealth of experience to the commission's deliberations.

Typically, they also bring a history of being involved in politics and a wide network of associations. They must be willing to cease any and all political activity during their time of service, including making contributions, and recuse themselves from cases in which they know their judgment would be compromised by personal relationships.

Sadly, many commissioners have looked across the table at relatives, former business associates, and people who were members of their wedding parties. The vote to refer a case for criminal prosecution is public, with commissioners either raising their hands or voting by voice in the presence of the accused. It takes *gravitas* both to vote and to recuse oneself from voting. There were instances, Jimmy says, in which he was the *only* commissioner on the five-person panel to vote. Imagine being the only person to decide that the person across the table is going to be criminally prosecuted!

Jimmy had only been a commissioner for four months when a grand jury (not the Ethics Commission but one generated by an earlier Ethics Commission inquiry) indicted Governor Hunt for spending $200,000 from a 1987 inaugural account to purchase lawnmowers and marble showers. Hunt was found guilty and forced to resign on April 22, 1993. The state's Democratic lieutenant governor, Jim Jr., became Alabama's new governor. (Hunt never gave up insisting on his innocence, and in April 1998, after he had served his full sentence and paid his fine, the parole board pardoned him, believing in his innocence.)

Large sums of money were involved both in Governor Hunt's use of aircraft and his diversion of inaugural funds, but what immediately began to impress Jimmy, as he began listening to cases presented to the commission, was how little it often took to corrupt many public officials. A county commissioner who had served four or five terms—someone in a position to know better—might go off the rails for $2,500. In fact, the largest amount of money involved in a case to come before the commission in the last sixteen years was $18,500. (Federal investigators usually spot bigger cases long before they come to the Ethics Commission's attention.)

Yet dozens of public officials came before the Ethics Commission during Jimmy's tenure. Industrial relations director Dottie Cieszynski was eventually fined $3,000 in 1996 for using state employees for her personal errands and a state car for her personal use. Selma mayor Joe Smitherman was fined $4,000 in 1998 for using his city automobile to make personal trips to the beach. Former Birmingham Water Board chairman Horace Parker was convicted in 1998 for arranging to get a water main upgrade done on the street on which he lived in Gardendale to improve the water pressure for his lawn sprinkler system. Parker actually voted as a member of the water board to approve the work. While the deliberations of the

Ethics Commission are secret, their work in cases like these can be inferred from the resulting prosecutions and convictions.

Perhaps seven out of ten cases that come before the commission involve the use of public funds or position for one's personal benefit. Sex is involved in about two to three cases, as public officials promote, provide salary increases, or grant unusual freedoms to employees with whom they are having affairs.

Public officials are put in charge of large amounts of money that are not their own. They also direct staffs that fear their careers will be damaged by reporting misbehavior. They can grow to feel entitled to skirting the rules because, after all, they are doing so much good for so many.

These conditions make ethics violations widespread in public service. Jimmy came to understand how much worse public governance might be without watchdog groups like the Alabama Ethics Commission.

Jimmy served as chairman of the commission during the last year of his term, from September 1, 1996, through August 31, 1997 (although his service extended through March 5, 1998, when his successor was named by the state Senate). During that year, the director of the Ethics Commission, Melvin Cooper, decided to retire, and Jimmy led the search for his successor. He found an ideal candidate in the man we have been quoting, the current director of the Ethics Commission, Jim Sumner. A graduate of Samford University's law school, Sumner spent fifteen years in politics, rising to chief of staff of the state's attorney general before neutralizing himself politically by working as vice president for legislative affairs for the Alabama Hospital Association and subsequently representing the Alabama University System to the state legislature for ten years. He understood politics, state governance, public employment, and the state's vendors.

Through the interview process and during their short time of service together, Jim Sumner and Jimmy Pursell shared mutual concerns and became allies in reforms they thought the state needed. Sumner says that Jimmy remains an important person to the Ethics Commission and his influence continues well beyond his time of service. "Anyone who meets Jimmy Pursell just knows that ethics is in his DNA," Sumner says.

Jimmy's time on the commission and his general understanding of state governance caused him to realize that the most frequent and widespread abuse of the public trust never came before the commission because it was part of Alabama's standard operating procedure. Many people who worked for Alabama held more than one position. A county commissioner might also be the business manager of a municipality. A public school teacher might also be a state legislator. The usual procedure was for both jobs to pay the individual simultaneously when the person could not possibly attend to both sets of responsibilities at once. Schools just went on paying their teacher-legislators, for instance, when they vanished from the classroom during legislative sessions, even though the schools incurred the extra cost of hiring substitutes. In Jimmy's opinion, "double-dipping" was a real problem.

Double-dipping presented so much of a problem that no one wanted to take it on. During Jimmy's time of service on the Ethics Commission, the Ethics Commission could say nothing about the problem because no legislator was willing to ask the commission for a ruling on the question.

Jim Sumner and Jimmy Pursell talked about double-dipping, the commission's lack of subpoena power, and other limitations that made the commission less effective than it needed to be. As a result of these discussions, Jim Sumner and his staff began to construct a wish list of reforms.

In 2002, a legislator finally asked the commission for an opinion on double-dipping. The commission's advice was that any public official who was also an employee should not be paid for work that required a leave-of-absence. The public employee could only be paid simultaneously for both positions if the work (1) took place at a different time of day, as with a public school teacher who serves on a school board meeting in the evenings, or (2) if the public employee used sick days or vacation time to serve in a public office, or (3) if a flexible schedule could be arranged whereby the public employee met the same standard as others in his position as to number of hours worked. Otherwise, the public employee's compensation should be suspended for the time he served as a public official and vice versa.

The Ethics Commission's opinion took a long time to take hold among public officials. Indeed, it took a Pulitzer-prize-winning series in the *Birmingham News* by Brett J. Blackledge that showed just how far double-dipping could go. His research revealed that forty-three Alabama legislators held jobs within Alabama's two-year college system between 2002 and 2006. Most of these jobs were conferred on legislators after their election and were effectively no-show positions.

That still did not convince Alabama to be serious about systemic ethics reform. It took Governor Don Siegelman's conviction for accepting a $500,000 contribution or bribe from Richard Scrushy, CEO of HealthSouth, to keep his seat on Alabama's Certificate of Need Review Board in 2009.

The state's current double-dipping law, which follows the commission's reasoning, was finally passed in 2010 during a special legislative session called in December by outgoing Governor Riley. Other commission reforms were passed during that same session, including the granting of subpoena power to the Ethics Commission. In fact, Jim Sumner's wish list, formed in large part in consultation with Jimmy Pursell, helped shape the legislation.

From 1992–1997, Pursell Industries' POLYON® enjoyed a phenomenal run as the best controlled-release fertilizer on the market. The company had grown substantially to around $90 million in sales and was operating as two distinct divisions: consumer and technology. The consumer group was headed by Taylor and focused on selling retailers. The technology group was headed by David and sold to other fertilizer companies around the country. By now, POLYON® and SulfurKote were considered the top quality controlled-release fertilizer products in the country, and other fertilizer manufacturers needed them. Both Taylor and David reported to Jimmy.

Both divisions of the company were growing rapidly and needed capital to fund this growth. Jimmy had two good businesses and one pocketbook. In 1996, a public company approached the family and offered to buy the consumer products division.

Taylor, being young, felt that he had not accomplished what he wanted to in life and felt the consumer group had a lot more potential for growth. He also did not want to go to work for another company. He received permission to seek a partner to buy the consumer group from the family.

Taylor began working with investment bankers and interviewed various private equity groups as potential partners. Taylor met the partners of Citicorp Venture Capital, LTD (CVC), the private-equity arm of what is now CitiGroup and immediately felt that he had met his future partner.

In March of 1997, the consumer group was spun out of the family business in a leveraged buyout (LBO), a common practice used by private-equity firms. Taylor partnered with CVC in a mission to "roll up" the consumer lawn and garden business. The deal between CVC and the family included supply agreement with the technology group (now renamed Pursell Technologies) to purchase POLYON® for use in consumer products.

The consumer group, called Pursell Industries, grew via acquisition and organic growth to become the second-largest consumer fertilizer company in the world. This group supplied Home Depot, Lowe's, Kmart, Ace Hardware, True Value, and many other major retailers on a national basis and in Canada. This growth also benefited Pursell Technologies, as it meant much higher purchases of POLYON®. Spectrum Brands out of St. Louis later acquired the consumer group.

Jimmy renamed the remaining company Pursell Technologies, Inc. David Pursell was appointed president and CEO, and Jimmy became chairman of the board. The LBO of the consumer group allowed Pursell Technologies, Inc., to focus on its core business and continue to develop higher and higher quality controlled-release fertilizer technologies.

The sale to CVC happened as Jimmy was recruiting Jim Sumners to lead the Ethics Commission and conferring with him about what needed to be done to ensure good governance in Alabama. The Ethics Commission had given Jimmy a window on how little it can take to corrupt public officials—or let their tendency to corruption emerge. His time on the commission would soon be at an end, and he wanted to keep on doing something in his home state to address the problem.

One of Jim Sumner's solutions was education. He led the Ethics Commission in a new effort to reach public officials and inform them of their ethical responsibilities. Since he became director of the Ethics Commission, he and his team have led fifty to sixty seminars for small groups of public officials each year in the state's ethics law.

Jimmy thought he might do something with an even more enduring impact. As a consultant, Achilles Armenakis had helped Jimmy reform the governance of his company in a way that prepared for the growth that followed. Armenakis was a specialist in corporate change. From the first time that Armenakis met with Jimmy and saw the plaque on Jimmy's wall from the Fellowship of Companies for Christ, he knew that his work with Jimmy would be unlike anything he had previously experienced. That had been validated time and again. As an active layman in a Greek Orthodox Church, Armenakis found Jimmy's beliefs and the way these had changed his company attractive. Armenakis's insights into how a company can initiate changes that become institutionalized had been validated time and again. Jimmy wondered whether ethical changes might come about in companies in a similar way. He thought Achilles Armenakis was the right person to find out.

In 1998, Jimmy and Chris Pursell endowed the James T. Pursell Sr. Eminent Chair in business ethics at Auburn University, with Achilles Armenakis its first recipient. Jimmy and Chris also supplied funds for a Distinguished Fellows in Ethics program that would bring high-profile figures who had made crucial ethical stands to the Auburn campus. Roger Boisjoly who warned against the O-ring problem that caused the Shuttle *Challenger* disaster was the first distinguished fellow. Dr. Jeffrey Wigand, who exposed the tobacco industry's long-concealed knowledge of their products, devastating effects, was the second. In recent years Jimmy's involvement with the Ethics Commission has circled back to Auburn, as Jay Grinney, the CEO brought in at HealthSouth to clean up the Scrushy/Siegelman mess, lectured, followed by the Ethics Commission's own Jim Sumner. At the time when Jimmy established the chair in business ethics, there wasn't a course at Auburn in ethics outside of the philosophy department. The teaching of ethics has now been integrated into the curriculum throughout Auburn's outstanding Raymond J. Harbert College of Business, with the entire Auburn community benefitting from the Distinguished Fellows in Ethics program.

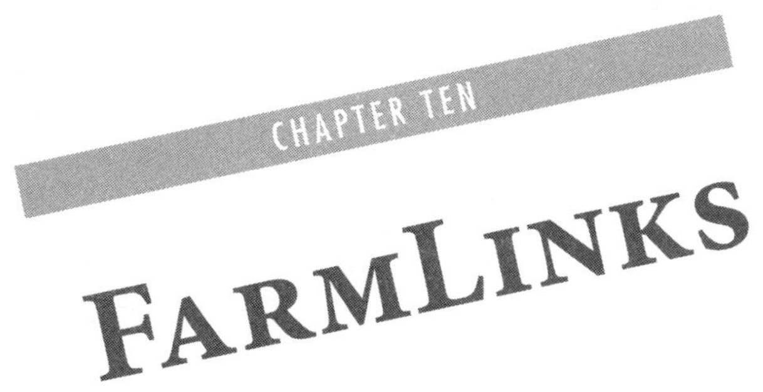

With the division of the company into Pursell Industries and Pursell Technologies, Inc., in 1997, strategic decisions needed to be made. The first consideration was office space. The corporate offices were then located in downtown Sylacauga, but the division of the company and its personnel suggested a move would be in order. As the new president and CEO of Pursell Technologies, David Pursell scouted other locations. The first one that seemed promising demanded the creation of infrastructure—roads built, the extension of utility connections, etc. If the company would have to spend that type of money, then David felt free to suggest an alternative he had in mind.

Jimmy and Chris's life, and the life of David's family, was by now established at Pennywinkle Farm, the name Chris has given to the property that Jimmy had added to through the years around the Old Hamilton Place. Pennywinkle Farm had grown to some three thousand five hundred acres, from the stream-fed pastureland along the base of Chalybeate Mountain all the way to its forested top. Pennywinkle Farm was now, in fact, the largest cattle ranch in the county.

David, Ellen, and their children lived across the street from one entrance and Jimmy and Chris from another. Groups of distributors and their potential customers—six at a time—were actively being hosted in the Hamilton Place's guest house. It made sense to David to establish the corporate offices of Pursell Technologies at the farm, which was only a fifteen-minute drive from downtown Sylacauga. Jimmy agreed. But David soon had another idea, which Jimmy questioned.

David and his family spent a lot of time on the farm, roaming over the property on four-wheelers. So had Jimmy. Both men loved the property with tremendous passion.

For Jimmy, the farm's particular appeal lay both in its beauty—the green tree-lined pastures underneath the sheltering mountain that purpled at dusk—and its history, as old railway lines traced through it and there was an earthen-works that Jimmy believed could have been constructed by the explorer DeSoto. David appreciated these things as well, but he also noted the land's variety, as it included several mini-ecosystems, not only pastures and forest but wetlands as well. Ripples from the upheaval that had created the Appalachians gave the acreage at Chalybeate Mountain's base a complex of rises and falls that created vantage points everywhere on the property. The farm had its own natural divisions and a surprising variety of landscapes.

From the first days that David and Ellen established residence across the street from the farm, David would sit on the porch in the evenings and imagine how golf holes might be constructed on the family's land. At other times, bouncing over the property on a four-wheeler, he would stop on a rise and imagine a tee box there and how the fairway below would stretch out to a well-bunkered green.

David knew these to be idle dreams, however. The farm, located in the two-gas-station town of Fayetteville, was at least a forty-five-minute drive across the mountains from Birmingham, the closest population center with enough golfers to support what he had in mind.

The Lowe's visit and all that followed as the company learned how to market POLYON® through combining Southern hospitality with customer-education turned David's musings about building a golf course in a more serious direction. After all, golf courses were POLYON®'s best customers. They played golf with their customers before educating them about the product. They had even been embarrassed on one memorable occasion to find a competitor's product being used at a course where they took their potential clients. David began dreaming of building a golf course that could be a showcase for POLYON®. The groups could play on fairways and greens that were living demonstrations of POLYON®'s benefits! They could even use POLYON® on one side of the fairway and a competitor's product on the other—or on alternate holes. (Both strategies were, in fact, eventually employed.) David remembered the old proverb, "I was told and I forgot. I saw and I remembered. I did and I understood." The Pursell Technologies experience would be like no other. The company's educational sessions could simply demonstrate why POLYON® worked and explain its long-term cost advantages.

Still, David understood that golf courses are hugely expensive propositions. The initial capital investment represented only a portion of what was needed. The greater challenge would be maintenance. The land sat on top of a substantial aquifer that could be tapped for water. Fertilizer was a given. But the year-round maintenance crews, customer service staffing, groundskeeping equipment, additional landscaping, golf carts, sod, sand, etc.—the yearly costs would run into the millions and the purpose of the course would be defeated if it weren't immaculately maintained. Pursell Technologies had some money in its pocket from the sale of Pursell Industries, but not nearly enough for such an ambitious undertaking.

The obvious challenges did not stop David. He saw that the utility of such a golf course to Pursell Technologies as a marketing vehicle would apply to other suppliers in the golf course industry, if he could recruit them as partners.

Prudently, David had become involved in the Golf Course Superintendents Association of America. The friends he made through the association gave him a wide-ranging network throughout the golf industry. His guiding idea of building the world's first research-and-demonstration golf course on the family farm engaged his distinctive leadership abilities. His wife, Ellen, has pointed out that David's leadership style differs from the "type-A" personalities of the world, who lead by creating a flurry of enthusiasm and dominate those around them. David's strengths lie in an imaginative grasp of possibilities others don't see, complemented by seeking the counsel of a wide-ranging group of people and an unremitting persistence in working through the details of a problem. These abilities stamped what would become the Experience at FarmLinks customer trips with David's trademark.

David began speaking with golf course architects, contractors who had experience building courses, and leaders of companies who might join with Pursell Technologies in maintaining the course once it was built.

In many ways the tone of the project was established by building the new corporate office building and a lodge for additional guests. Jimmy, and even more so his wife, Chris, wanted the land disturbed as little as possible and everything built on the farm to be unobtrusive and fit well with the landscape. They wanted whatever construction projects were undertaken to maintain the feel of being down home in Alabama. Anyone who travels around the Sylacauga area can see why. There's a surprising amount of industry, much of it due to the high-grade marble quarried in the area. The columns of the capitol in Washington, DC; the Lincoln Memorial; and the Supreme Court Building were made out of marble from Sylacauga. The plants that service the area's industries are built on tracks of bottomland that have been bulldozed flat and bald and constructed with no consideration save utility. They are just like plants everywhere else in America, but in the middle of the bucolic Alabama countryside they seem particularly monstrous and alien.

The office building for Pursell Technologies was built on a tree-covered rise. It's a large building, covering twenty-two thousand square feet. Yet most of the building is all but invisible. Trees surround the back of the building, concealing most of the space from view. The front entrance at the top of the drive looks modest at most.

Parker Lodge has a more dramatic rock façade, in the style of a Colorado resort, but again its true dimensions are concealed as it is hangs dramatically on the side of a cliff, with only its entrance at the top.

Parker Lodge made it possible to expand tremendously the Pursell Technologies Incorporated tour for distributors and their clients. It doubled the opportunity to begin hosting the retreats of the many ministries they were already working with and to significantly expand the list. Jimmy's commitment to running his company for Christ expanded through hospitality. The Pursells had always invited people out to the farm for fishing in its ponds and company picnics, but now they could invite groups far and wide to make use of Parker Lodge's facilities. Both Jimmy and David cherished this new opportunity.

David hoped to use the golf course design firm Hurdzan/Fry because of their sensitivity to the natural landscape. Unlike other architects of the golf world who build dramatic courses on plain land by moving as much dirt as necessary, Hurdzan/Fry specializes in creating challenging golf courses while impacting the environment as little as possible. What David had in mind would be an ideal project for their approach.

Through his networking, David made a breakthrough with Toro, one of the largest suppliers of groundskeeping equipment to golf courses. They saw the advantages of becoming a partner in the proposed research-and-demonstration course. The future Pursell Technologies Customer Tours would give thousands of golf course superintendents the opportunity to test-drive their mowers and other equipment. Toro had a compatible culture with Pursell Technologies, as their sales approach stressed both personal relationships and education, but they had nothing like the proposed golf course as a venue. Their greatest concern was the longevity of the payoff. Would their participation in the project continue to be beneficial five years down the road? They became convinced it would.

After Toro, Club Car came on board, then Syngenta and others.

Still, these parties were only interested if and when the course was actually built. Jimmy continued to have reservations. Chris did not want to see anything on the farm but more cows.

For this reason, David would go only so far in advancing the idea with his father and allowed for four years to pass, giving the idea time to either mature or die. Jimmy and David agreed on the bottom-line criterion of whether to build the golf course. Would it allow them to "sell mo' fuh-tuh-lizuh"?

Jimmy finally decided it would.

David informed the Pursell Technologies staff of the ambitious plan in an email memo. The staff was generally excited by the prospect but skeptical that their small company could pull it off.

The bulldozers began moving dirt late in the summer of 2001.

Then the terrorist attack of 9/11 happened.

The whole golf course industry held its breath. Many projects were put on hold or suspended indefinitely.

Pursell Technologies took a long, hard look at whether to continue. Jimmy and David decided to take the risk.

Once Jimmy decided that the golf course should be built, he committed himself to the project wholeheartedly. He even revealed a secret of the property that became the signature fifth hole. He knew a waterfall existed opposite the cliff on which the hole was built—one that was usually covered by bushes growing up over the rock face but ran nearly the entire year nevertheless. He pointed this out to the golf architects, who then removed enough of the surrounding vegetation to expose the fall's brilliance. They stationed the tee box for number five on part of the surrounding cliff and placed the green at the bottom of the ravine in front of the waterfall. Golfers would have a spectacular view from the tee box and also face a dizzying shot as the hole fell away one hundred seventy feet to the green below.

Jimmy kept close tabs on how number five developed—once, too close. When the hole was still being built and the service road to the tee box but a slim dirt path, he drove his Lexus up the precipice and stepped up for a look. It only took one step off the dirt road before the drop-off set him running to regain his balance. Tilted too far forward to slide on his bottom, he kept crashing forward until he landed face down on rocky ground. Number five sent him to the hospital and through a long, sore recovery. For his pains, he found the staff had named the hole "Jimmy's Falls."

The property presented many advantages but also difficulties. Land that's been used over generations to pasture cows is rife with every type of weed known to man. Pennywinkle Farms also hosted a plague-like population of armyworms. The workers who seeded the greens and sprigged the fairways would look out over their handiwork only to see the land rippling with the scourge. Usually by the time they arrived, crows covered the ground, feasting on the black mess. Vast invading forces of armyworms appeared in one place one day, another the next. Their populations were supposed to peak in late August, but the summer the fairways went in, they came on early in late June, as the result of wet weather, and stayed for the season.

In most places, the farm had eighteen inches of incredibly rich topsoil, but the dramatic eighteenth fairway that would seep up to the clubhouse was next to wetlands. There the soil was dense, hard clay. It became saturated with rain or irrigation and then baked hard quickly—neither condition encouraged grass to germinate and grow. It would ultimately be planted three times with two different kinds of grass before establishing itself.

Chris remained fierce in her defense of trees. How fierce, one worker discovered soon after joining the crew.

It's impossible to maintain closely mown grass around mature trees. For this reason, large buffers of treeless areas were needed around the greens. A new worker found himself struggling to establish a particular green and marked additional trees for cutting. On his way to another location on the property, he passed Jimmy and Chris, who were out for a walk. They exchanged pleasantries and went their separate ways. When he came back to the same green, he found someone—very likely Chris—had removed the flags on the trees he wanted cut. He would have to find another way to get that green to flourish.

Cost overruns on golf courses are typical, as no one can predict the weather, the soil conditions everywhere on a property, and how an architect's design may translate into reality. It often seems like a good idea to move some additional dirt for a side mound that will vary shots from the fairway or place a hitherto unthought-of bunker beneath a green's false front. It's easy to get carried away improving the design and blowing the budget sky high as a result. Many leaders with big ideas hate details and don't want to be bothered with too many day-to-day decisions, but David Pursell stayed on top of the golf course project throughout. He and his team built the course close to budget. His father always told him, "You have to earn your wings," and David knew that's a lifelong process.

His efforts paid off in a golf course that has been rated the number-one public-access course in Alabama and found its way onto *Golf Digest*'s "Top 75 Resort Courses in North America." The course manages to be both a demanding test for skilled golfers and forgiving for neophytes—or those who only play once or twice a year at company outings. From the tips, the course measures over 7,400 yards, and the eighteenth hole, a par five, plays a long 616 yards uphill. But there are five sets of tee boxes that progressively cut down the length and confine the mandatory carries almost exclusively to the par threes. The fairways are generous—the eighteenth fairway is over 60 yards wide at one point, in fact, although there's a tree in the middle of it, demanding the golfer pick a line, right or left. Those who are prone to top their drives can generally find them and hit again without penalty, unlike many contemporary "target courses" that demand the ball fly a certain distance before the fairway begins. It's what golfers call a "second-shot course," as the bent grass greens are large but dramatically sloped and fast. It's best to keep the ball below the hole or the golfer may face a long downhiller that can roll right off the green. This places a premium on the golfer's short game and proves one of the principles of legendary golf instructor Harvey Penick that "a golfer who can chip and putt can play with any man." Those who can no longer hit it a mile can still empty their competitor's pockets!

As the course was being finished, David Pursell and his team searched for a perfect name. David hit upon "FarmLinks," a nice pairing of its binary nature. David also came up with the concept for the course's logo, a Longhorn bull dressed like Bobby Jones in a tie, posing at the moment of finishing a golf shot. It suggests, as people used to say, that "golf is a gentleman's game," and one that requires passion. Or, as the old saying goes, "Golf isn't any fun unless you take it seriously, and if you do, it will break your heart."

Very few hearts are broken at FarmLinks, however. Turning off of Talladega Springs Road onto wood-fenced-lined Farmlinks Boulevard—the main entrance into the property—brings with it a welcome and even uncanny sense of entering into a downhome preserve of peace and tranquility. There are pastures on either side, where Longhorn cattle graze, before the drive passes through stands of trees that then open up to reveal the first of the course's spectacular golf holes. Along the way to the clubhouse, the drive passes Lake Christine—one of Pursell Farm's best fishing places—more forested areas and more of the golf course until ending at the clubhouse—once again, a building that looks like a snug Alabama frame house while containing a gourmet restaurant and, on the backside lower level, the cart house. The drive into the property is at once dramatic and soothing. It feels like leaving one's cares behind for an experience that's going to be absorbing and wonderful, just as many people have found it.

FarmLinks opened as the world's first—and only—research-and-demonstration golf facility in 2003. The governor of Alabama and many dignitaries attended the opening day festivities. Jimmy's now-famous childhood friend, Jim Nabors, was there to entertain. More than anything, what most people took away from that day, including the crew who had built the course, was the way that Jimmy and Chris welcomed everyone, just as if they had been personally invited into the Pursells' home. That's really what the farm was, of course. But while many people might be inclined to become more standoffish at the prospect of having a continual flow of golfers as guests, Jimmy and Chris's openness gave the impressive operation a mom-and-pop feel. Still today, Jimmy greets everyone in the clubhouse at lunchtime like a long-lost friend. It's quickly apparent how Jimmy converted his customers over the years into friends.

Opening Day was particularly satisfying for David Pursell as well.

But would they "sell mo' fuh-tuh-lizuh"? That they did, and in incredible abundance. An early survey found that the Experience at FarmLinks turned nearly 100 percent of visitors into POLYON® buyers. The only holdout couldn't help it, as he had run into trouble with the law and was then in jail!

The success of FarmLinks as a business venture opened up new opportunities for Christian ministry and charity work as well. In fact, over the succeeding years, the property has averaged hosting over forty non-profit endeavors per year. These include a first-tee program for children;

a program for promising young Christian leaders around the world called The Leadership Institute; and Vapor International, a program that builds self-sustaining centers in third-world countries to make disciples, provide humanitarian aid, and disseminate disease-prevention education. Vapor's headquarters is located right across from the entrance to Pursell Farms.

One of the ministries that has meant the most to David Pursell is Bruce Johnston's JH Ranch. The ministry began by hosting weeklong adventures for parents and teens at the JH Ranch in northern California. It has since expanded into Outback America, a weekend program primarily for parents and their teenaged children, and Outback University for college-age students. Through music and drama, inspiring talks, small-group sessions, and lots of outdoor activities, family members are encouraged to connect with God as a means of reconnecting with one another. It's all about relationships, just as the Pursell family has always been. David helped Bruce Johnston start the Birmingham chapter. While golf isn't part of the program, the farm provides plenty of room for the tents that host the participants and all their outdoor activities.

Through the years, Jimmy and Chris were always seeking ways to use the farm for God's purposes. Long before FarmLinks came into existence, they started what was called the "Committee for Farm Ministry." Building the golf course exponentially opened up the possibilities of using the property for ministry.

CHAPTER ELEVEN

An Ever-Expanding Legacy

When Jimmy Pursell committed himself and then his company to Christ, he began sharing his newfound spiritual enthusiasm with those closest to home, with his family, his close friends, his employees, and the people in Sylacauga. He shared it with the toughest crowds of all, really, since these people could see the consistency of his witness and judge whether he remained faithful to it over the long term. He put into practice immediately what Bruce Wilkinson would later recommend as the appropriate pattern for Christian business owners. His service to others continued to ripple outward and acquired, in due time, an international dimension as well, as we saw in the "prayer of Canton" episode; Chris and he were examining how they might help Christians in China at the time that the first SCU plant came online.

Jimmy and Chris's interest in international ministry has been extended through their children. Aaron and Chrissy's church in Montgomery placed a particular emphasis on missionary outreach. And David, among other initiatives, gave Vapor International a home base at Pursell Farms.

Jimmy's legacy will also extend through those whom he has worked with, especially a man named Dr. Amit Roy, who is working on the problem of world hunger.

Almost all of the fertilizer technologies in the world were developed in Muscle Shoals, Alabama, after World War I. Muscle Shoals is located on the Tennessee River and is also the location of a large hydroelectric dam (Wilson Dam).

At the outset of World War I, President Woodrow Wilson ordered the construction of two nitrate plants that would be powered by Wilson Dam. The nitrates would be used to produce munitions for the war effort. Nitrates are the building block for bombs and also fertilizers. Ammonium nitrate is a widely used nitrogen fertilizer.

After the war, the government decided to utilize these same facilities to go from "swords to plowshares" and implement the largest research program ever conducted on fertilizers in the world. Populations were rising rapidly. Many parts of the world had extreme famines. The world had to grow more food.

This initiative was implemented under the Tennessee Valley Authority (TVA) and called the National Fertilizer Development Center (NFDC). It was a massive undertaking. During the 1970s there were more chemical engineers in Muscle Shoals, Alabama, than in any city on earth. John Shields led this amazing effort.

By chance, Jimmy's fertilizer business was the closest fertilizer company to Muscle Shoals and became the "guinea pig" to try out new products developed by NFDC. This actually became a competitive advantage for the company, as Jimmy forged a very close working relationship and friendship with these people. NFDC had the brightest people they could find working on very complex technologies. Jimmy's company would often see new technologies well before others and oftentimes purchased the first production runs of these new materials, as with the first SCU products.

He also realized how important NFDC's work could be in solving hunger issues around the world.

Over time, the NFDC transitioned to an international development organization. In 1974, Henry Kissinger addressed the United Nations and proposed an international effort to improve agricultural production for developing countries through better access and property use of improved fertilizer technologies. President Carter conveyed the Public International Organization status to the new International Fertilizer Development Center (IFDC). IFDC enjoys the same diplomatic status as the United Nations and the World Bank, something unheard of in Alabama. In fact, these are the only three in the United States! IFDC has worked in over one hundred countries and currently has offices in twenty-six countries around the world. IFDC is crucial to global food security.

The CEO of IFDC is Jimmy Pursell's longtime collaborator, Dr. Amit Roy. Amit grew up in India and graduated from the Indian Institute of Technology (one in ten thousand are accepted). Amit came to the United States to get his PhD at Georgia Tech in chemical engineering with a focus on fertilizer technology. After Georgia Tech, Amit spent his entire career at IFDC. Amit and Jimmy are close friends and have worked together for many years, as IFDC was instrumental in the development of SCU.

Amit told Jimmy that his goal for IFDC was to revolutionize agricultural fertilizers the way Jimmy had revolutionized specialty fertilizers (for golf courses, consumer products, etc.). What Amit meant was that agricultural fertilizers are very inefficient. Most of the nitrogen fertilizers applied in the world are lost as runoff into lakes and streams. Realizing the importance of technological development, Amit developed a research initiative to create a new class of fertilizers that were "timed release" like POLYON®, only focused on agricultural crops, such as rice and corn, instead of turf. These products are also designed to be very low cost to a poor farmer in a developing country. These products require *less fertilizer* and *improve yields by 35 percent or more*. The results are very promising. To date, these products have contributed over $700 million towards poverty reduction over the past three years in Bangladesh alone.

The world will have to grow twice as much food as today by 2050. This is due to a growing population (9.6 billion by 2050), biofuels (food turned into fuel), and changing diets (more meat consumption). Most folks don't know that it takes eight pounds of corn to grow one pound of beef. The fertilizer technology does not exist today to grow this much food. Amit's vision to help solve this problem was inspired by Jimmy Pursell's innovations in new, controlled-release fertilizer technologies. A wonderful legacy to leave that could positively impact millions around the world.

In 2005, three different companies approached Jimmy Pursell and David Pursell about acquiring Pursell Technologies, Inc. With the success of FarmLinks as the only research-and-development course in the nation and with hundreds and then thousands of wholesale distributors, nursery chains, and golf superintendents having become devoted customers of POLYON® via the FarmLinks Tour, PTI was a dominant player in the American market with a growing presence internationally. It also had an immaculate balance sheet. Even the FarmLinks golf course was completely paid off.

PTI did not have the capital resources of the international giants in their industry, of course. They were still dwarfed by PotashCorp, Mosaic, CF Industries, and others. They were large enough, however, to pose a real challenge to these companies and so began facing the compliment of "imitation." Products began appearing on the market that were suspiciously like POLYON®. A Canadian-based company, Agrium, one of the world's top ten fertilizer manufacturers, wanted to improve its own programmable, time-release products. They were doing well with a product for broad acre applications but wanted to improve the sophistication of their own technology and expand into POLYON®'s markets. Agrium emerged as the leading bidder for PTI.

David Pursell conducted the negotiations, with Jimmy staying in the background. This was strategic. Jimmy's absence from the negotiating table automatically paced the negotiations to PTI's liking. They couldn't be caught up in a session where they might get steamrolled. Even more importantly, David was able to play good cop to Jimmy's bad cop. "I don't know if my father is going to go for that!" he would say, shaking his head. ("Hick" country boys have been using the same tactics to skin alive emissaries from the "big city" for generations!) All the time, of course, Jimmy and David were on the same page as to what they wanted and conferred continually as the negotiations progressed.

On August 6, 2006, Agrium, Inc., announced that it had "concluded the purchase of certain fixed assets and inventory of Pursell Technologies, Inc. and certain of its affiliates." With everything added in, the purchase price was close to nine figures. At the same time, Jimmy and his family did not give up all of their proprietary technologies. They retained the results of a number of their research projects because, as Jimmy had learned so well, new technologies can transform existing commodities into transformational products. The family also retained the FarmLinks golf course and all the property associated with Pursell Farms. Agrium became a new partner in the use of FarmLinks, running what it came to call Agrium University—a somewhat broader-based marketing and educational program—out of the farm's demonstration center. Other companies began renting the facilities for similar purposes as well.

No one knew this at the time, of course, but the financial crash of 2008 was close at hand. David and Jimmy sold PTI at an optimal time. Once again, Jimmy's business seems to have been providentially blessed.

The sale enabled Jimmy to do even more to leaven American business with ethical corporate cultures. Once again he approached his long-time colleague and friend Achilles Armenakis about expanding the ethics program within Auburn's business college. In 1998, we recall, Jimmy endowed the James T. Pursell Eminent Scholar Chair at Auburn, to which Achilles was the first appointed, as well as the James T. Pursell Sr. Eminent Scholars Program. For nearly ten years, the program, administered by Achilles, had been bringing people who "spoke truth to power," such as Roger Boisjoly, who warned of the problems with O-rings that resulted in the *Challenger* Shuttle disaster, and Jeff Wigand, who exposed the tobacco industry's knowledge—which it had repeatedly denied, even in congressional hearings—that its products were not only addictive but expressly engineered to be as addictive as possible.

Jimmy wanted to start a program whereby a company—any company, whether it was run by Christians or not—could be assessed as to its ethical standing. Achilles had helped Jimmy improve his business's operations, and in doing so had also helped Parker Fertilizer (which then became Pursell Industries and later Pursell Technologies, Inc.) to live out its dedication to Christ. Could not a system be devised that would enable other companies at least to understand whether they were doing business in an ethical way? The 2000s saw company after company run afoul of the law and blow up as a business, including Enron and, in Jimmy's Alabama, HealthSouth, run by the now infamous Richard Scrushy. Many similar stories would unfortunately soon follow.

Achilles put together a plan for the James T. Pursell Sr. Center for Ethical Organizational Cultures. Jimmy liked everything about the plan except for the name. He did not want the center to be seen as his but Auburn's—a project to which Auburn as an institution would be firmly committed over the long haul. At Jimmy's insistence, the name was changed to The Auburn University Center for Ethical Organizational Cultures.

Starting in 2008, the center began supporting three faculty members as well as five PhD students. Together, the center's faculty and graduate students conduct research on how corporations can function ethically and post the results of doing so. For example, one PhD candidate turned a quantitative assessment instrument as to the safety of a workplace into an instrument that provides quantitative data on the ethical practices (or lack thereof) of corporations.

This is now used, along with the interview method that Achilles Armenakis employed, as a first model of ethical assessment. Jimmy's own company served as the guinea pig for ethical assessment. Armenakis, following work that had already been done in the field, as we have seen, examined Jimmy's company on the basis of interviews with participants.

He also looked at three important criteria: (1) "artifacts in view"—in the case of Jimmy's company, there were Bibles on many desks and plaques on the wall attesting to the company's Christian commitment; (2) espoused beliefs—usually in the form of mission statements; and (3) underlying assumptions.

At Pursell Technologies, one person called the Bible the "company handbook." The heart of the company's mission statement was the Golden Rule—treat others as one would like to be treated. And when Achilles put Jimmy's managers in a room to discuss the significance of the artifacts found around the office, he found one incredibly strong underlying assumption: "The Bible is the Word of God." With a foundation like that, any unethical behavior would have to defy deliberately the ethical culture of the company.

As Achilles and his colleagues have continued to assess companies and teach students, they have found the "stakeholder management model" extremely helpful. Although libertarians like the late Harold Friedman denied that corporations could, in any sense, be considered "persons with moral responsibilities" or even "personal" and preached that the only purpose of a company was to make money, Achilles Armenakis and his colleagues believe that companies do have moral responsibilities. They are obligated not only to make a return on investment for their investors but also to treat their employees fairly, abide by all government regulations, and make contributions, both through volunteering and donations, to the communities in which they do business.

The Center for Ethical Organizational Cultures has also found, as one might suspect, that the compensation structure of a company wields the most powerful of all influences in creating an ethical or unethical environment. The financial disaster of 2008 was created in large part—at least in the investment and banking sectors—by compensation structures in which remuneration became less and less about serving clients and more and more about serving the financial institution's own interests, even if clients suffered as a result.

The research now coming from The Center for Ethical Organizational Cultures is as rigorous as any in academia but also unlike what nearly all secular universities produce. Consider the following current research project from Alan G. Walker of Auburn University and James W. Smither of La Salle University called "Sanctifying Work: Effects on Job Outcomes beyond Positive Affectivity and Core-Evaluations." In the studies abstract, they state:

> Sanctification involves perceiving objects or events theistically by viewing them as having spiritual significance and with reference to a higher being (i.e., God). Previous research has found positive outcomes associated with sanctification . . . Recently, Walker, Jones, Wuensch, & Cope (2008) extended these results into the world of work and found that those employees who sanctified their jobs were more satisfied, more committed to their organization, and at the same time, were less likely to intend to leave their current organization.
>
> This study seeks to further explore the importance of sanctification to these job outcomes by examining whether sanctification explains unique variance in job satisfaction . . . over and above variance explained by an overall positivity (as measured by the PANAS) and/or being well-adjusted, positive, confident, efficacious, and having belief in one's own agency (i.e., possessing high core self-evaluations).

In other words, does dedicating one's work to God make work more satisfying than simply having a positive attitude and belief in one's own abilities? It's a fascinating topic, and one that's unlikely to be investigated at Yale.

Achilles Armenakis says that the center operates on the "missionary model." Year after year, Auburn will produce newly minted PhDs who then export the center's concentration on ethical corporate cultures. This is already happening. One of the most promising developments involves the Air Force Academy, to which one PhD candidate will be returning to teach business ethics. One might not think this is as necessary at the Air Force

Academy as at other educational institutions, since the armed services have high ethical standards. Anyone following the news in recent years, however, will recognize, on second thought, that the Air Force has been experiencing significant ethical problems, particularly with sexual assaults on campus. Recently, the Navy has also shown interest in the center.

The family farm, with its FarmLinks golf course, has now officially become Pursell Farms (www.pursellfarms.com/). Its attractions as an outstanding resort, featuring clay shooting, bird hunting in season, fishing, and fine dining, as well as golf, are refocusing the Pursell family, particularly David Pursell and his team, on hospitality as a business. Hospitality is a Christian virtue that played a crucial role in converting the world to Christ in the first centuries of the Christian era. What could be more appropriate for Jimmy and his family, who have always put relationships first, both in life and business, as they have sought to serve God? They are making the heart and soul of what it's meant to be a Pursell into an occupation—as well as part of Jimmy's enduring legacy.

Jimmy Pursell has won many awards and been appointed to high positions, including his service on the board of the Fellowship of Companies for Christ International and the Alabama Ethics Commission.

In 2012, Auburn University's College of Human Sciences presented Jimmy and Chris Pursell with its Lifetime Achievement Award. Acknowledging their contributions, Auburn said:

> Success is measured by embodying the values of *hard work, education, love of country, obedience to law, and soundness of mind, body, and spirit* . . . Jimmy and Chris Pursell, as individuals and as a couple, are the gold standard for what it truly means to live the exemplary life . . . That is why the Auburn University College of Human Sciences proudly honors Jimmy and Chris Pursell with the 2012 Lifetime Achievement Award.

That's how Auburn University and other fine institutions measure success, but these standards, as important as they are, do not account for Jimmy's success nor the metrics he's chosen for his own life.

For the secret to Jimmy's success and Chris's life as well—lives that have influenced so many for good in such diverse ways—lies in the simplest and yet most radical action of all: the decision to obey God's call. Jimmy obeyed God when he heard God's call to give his company to Christ. He had as little idea of what this meant as Abraham did when God called him into a far country. Like Abraham, Jimmy did not know exactly where he was going, how he would get there, or what the risks entailed. He wondered, like the Old Testament patriarch—like every person of radical faith—whether the decision might simply be foolish. Nevertheless, he obeyed.

Obedience does not count for much with counselors, life coaches, and all the other peddlers of quick and easy transformation. Obedience does count with God, who alone knows the destiny for which He has made each of us. He alone can guide us there, step by step, often through the darkness of even the valley of death but never without reason or our ultimate good in mind. God alone knows what He means for our lives to become and how He intends to bless other people's lives through ours.

God is the ultimate multiplier. He takes five loaves and two fish and feeds five thousand. The seed He plants in good soil yields one hundredfold.

For God, as has often been said, anything is possible, even in tiny Sylacauga, Alabama. Because the center of God's universe is even smaller than the Sylacauga, Alabama, lying within each human heart. When someone like Jimmy turns to God with all his heart, the power that created the universe goes to work.

Jimmy Pursell is proof.

Family Tributes

APPENDIX 1

AIR JIMMY

BY TAYLOR PURSELL

No company has ever been able to make shoes large enough for my father to fit into. I have been told many times, "Taylor, you have some mighty big shoes to fill!" I quit trying a long, long time ago.

Dad likes everyone, and everyone likes Dad. I have never heard him say a negative thing about anyone. He received a very special gift from his parents (who were also like this) to be a magnet for people. That same trait is evident in his wonderful sister, my Aunt Dot (Dorothy Power). People just love to be around them because of the positive vibes they give off.

Dad is a natural athlete. He won the state hundred-yard dash in high school with a time of ten seconds flat. And this was forty years before Nike came on the scene with *real track shoes*. Dad became a legend because of his speed—something that almost did him in one afternoon. Dad was hanging around downtown Talladega one day during his high school days, when suddenly everyone starting screaming, "The convict has escaped the jail!" He looked up and saw a huge man running away down the railroad tracks. The police were in pursuit. Dad immediately took off after him as well. The only problem was that, due to his speed, *Dad caught up with him before the police did!* The closer he got, the bigger he saw the man was! Dad immediately smiled at the man and scaled back into a jog. No one else was even close.

Dad is a person of ultimate integrity. For years he has told me, "Always tell the truth so you don't have to remember what you said." It is very hard to remember a lie. Years ago I was in some litigation and spent a lot of time being deposed and listening to others being deposed. The folks on the other side were "prepped" by their lawyers for three days each! I just had a cup of coffee with my lawyer. There was nothing to be prepped for. Just tell the truth. A pretty simple concept that my father used to his advantage all his life.

One of Dad's very best friends was a fellow named Jack Wright. Jack and Dad grew up together in Talladega in the 1930s and 1940s. Jack came from a wealthy family and had most anything he wanted. Dad, in contrast, had very little except his wonderful parents and sister. In high school, Jack developed polio and was paralyzed below the waist. One of my earliest memories was going to Jack's house with my folks to visit. I remember Dad pushing Jack's wheelchair around and picking him up to put him in the car. They remained extremely close until Jack's death in 2000. The polio and the disability never affected their friendship.

Dad's closest friend has always been Jimmy Nabors. Jimmy has very similar "nice-guy" traits to my father. Jimmy would come visit Sylacauga often during his Hollywood heyday and would always spend time with Dad. They would immediately start recalling stories from high school and college and laugh all night long. Dad could literally not talk for days after Jimmy left town due to laughing so hard!

"Always hire folks around you that are smarter than you." Well, for me, this was not difficult to do. For Dad, it was tough. Dad learned a great lesson from my grandfather Howard Parker Sr. (Mom's father). When Dad joined the company just out of the Air Force, it was very small. Most of the business was conducted within a few adjacent counties. And being in agriculture, the business was very seasonal, meaning that for a good bit of the year there was nothing to do but sit around. My grandfather knew well that a company is only as good as its people, and he devised a way to hire the brightest people available by giving them a job *and* encouraging them to excel at something else during the slower times of the year. Dad started a billboard company and was literally making more money on the side than he was in his real job. And this was done with my grandfather's blessing and encouragement.

The same was done for Bill Nichols (my godfather). My grandfather hired Bill after World War II as an agronomist and sales person. Bill had been captain of Auburn's football team before being drafted into the Army. He came home from Germany with only one leg. Bill was encouraged by my grandfather to get into politics. He served eleven terms in the US Congress and was chairman of several of the most important congressional committees.

Dad took this same approach and began hiring overqualified people when he took over. I remember many going-away parties for people who made big steps up in their careers with new jobs or buying companies, all with Dad's encouragement and support. To Dad, happiness has always been to help someone succeed.

And there's my Mom. She is the feisty one! They always say opposites attract. On the inside, Mom and Dad are just alike, kind, outgoing, wonderful people. When one of the kids whined too much or got in trouble, Dad would stay calm and try to settle down the situation. Mom, on the other had, would "nip it in the bud" with one look (or swipe)! I remember the day my mom and my aunt Judy (her sister) were chatting away on the screened-in porch at my grandmother's home in Sylacauga. It was at this time that my brother got upset about something and started raising Cain. Mom picked up the pitcher of lemonade they were drinking and poured the entire contents on his head. The floor of that screened-in porch is still sticky today!

My family has been extremely blessed. This does not mean that there were not some very hard times. On many occasions when there would be a crisis at the company, instead of losing his cool (which I never saw happen in my entire life), Dad would always say, "Well, we just have to turn that lemon into a lemonade." He has a great knack of turning something bad into a positive outcome.

Being an ex-Air Force navigator during the Korean War, Dad has always loved to fly. Since selling the company, his taste in aircraft has gone from 727s to Cessna Citation jets. Dad always loved to have the jets come to Sylacauga Airport to pick up Mom, Aunt Dot, Aunt Judy, Chris, and Aaron for one of their frequent mini-vacations.

Dad gave up drinking about forty years ago, and the well-stocked bars on the Citations go unused unless I happen to be on the plane. One day Dad and I were flying to Muscle Shoals to see a pilot-plant run on a new fertilizer technology we were working on. On the way back, Dad reached into the cooler to grab what he thought was a Diet Coke. Dad opened it and took a long swallow. Immediately his eyes became very large and startled! He looked at the can and realized he had just taken his first swig of beer in forty years. Not wanting to be seen with the beer (I was the only one on the plane), Dad immediately handed the open beer to the pilot. The pilot looked at Dad and said, "Do you mind if we land first?"

The one thing I am very glad of is that I never had to sell anything to my father. He is the toughest negotiator I have ever seen. He will fight for the very last penny. And because he is so nice, people never got mad at him even though he almost always ended up with the upper hand.

Years ago, Dad flew over to Mississippi to meet with the CEO of our largest supplier of raw materials. The CEO picked Dad up from the airport and brought him over to his well-appointed office. As they were walking in the front door, Dad looked down and saw a shiny penny. Coming from humble beginnings, Dad tried to pick it up and it wouldn't move! He then began to kick the penny to dislodge it. About that time the CEO grabbed Dad's arm and said, "Jimmy, I will gladly give you all the pennies you want; however, *that penny* is the first penny our company ever made. We embedded it in the front door for everyone to see, and we really want to keep it!"

Dad has a positive impact on everyone he interacts with. He always has. Folks visiting the farm will always see Mom and Dad having lunch in the clubhouse. Almost every week, I'll see someone who tells me that they met my dad and how overwhelmed they were with his personality and kindness.

Dad has been, and continues to be, extremely successful in business and in life. He has also been extremely generous with his time and money, getting most of his personal satisfaction and fulfillment by helping others. Dad's shoes are getting larger and larger every day and harder and harder to fill. One thing's for sure, if Nike ever comes out with a shoe that big, it will most certainly be called Air Jimmy!

APPENDIX 2

My Dad, the Encourager

BY CHRIS PURSELL FLEMING

Jim Pursell has been such a great encouragement to me, his only daughter and middle child. He has served as an example for many people through the years.

He has been one to seek out wisdom from many counselors, always wanting to do the right thing at the right time in the right way. As with all families and businesses, some times are better than others. He provided our family a lake house, where we spent a lot of time as a family during the summers, especially during my teen years. Every year, as long as I can remember, he has provided Auburn University football tickets so that our fall seasons are full of trips to home games, where we tailgate with family and friends. He encouraged me to go to college, which for us simply meant Auburn!

One of my first jobs as a teenager was working for Dad and the Parker Fertilizer Company doing miscellaneous projects earning minimum wage, which in 1972–1974 was $1.60 an hour. One project I remember was with my high school sorority, the Free Lancers. We were able to work as a club filling thousands of eight-ounce bottles with this "green stuff"—water-soluble plant food. It would totally make anything it touched permanently green! But that was such a fun job, and we used the money for our summer beach trip to Panama City.

I did other jobs, gathering a few friends to re-sticker hundreds of fertilizer bags that were priced incorrectly. It was during the winter break, and we would sit in a freezing, unheated warehouse, blowing out fog as we breathed, but that too was a fun job and helped the company. My brothers worked in the warehouse, loading fertilizer bags into trucks. But I only weighed ninety-five pounds, so no heavy lifting for me.

My plan was to go to college and get married early, just as my parents did, but I graduated with no prospect of a husband. So, the next thing was for me to get a job. After teaching for one semester in Sylacauga City Schools, Dad offered me a sales job selling Sta-Green fertilizer for our family company. That was a huge step for him, but it was such a great opportunity for me, making me get out, meet strangers, make cold calls, and learn the business. The first two years, I traveled around the state making sales to our customers, who mostly all knew Dad.

Still, I think Dad worried about his "little" daughter driving around who knows where, so he asked me to come back into the office to back up the "outside" sales force. That job really fit me well. A couple of years after college graduation, I bought myself a little house. Through the work I had been given and my earnings, I learned to manage my own home—all thanks to Dad.

I worked with my father for six years until getting married to Aaron Fleming, a pastor in Montgomery, Alabama.

As a young child, Mom and Dad had us in a small church, Sunday school, and youth group. We were more "socially" than "spiritually involved" at that time. But we were pretty faithful in attendance.

Then while I was in college, our entire family had a spiritual awakening over a four-year period. That was a turning point for us all. During those years, Dad's life was challenged spiritually. As a young believer, he made some big decisions and stepped out of his "comfort level" and committed the company to Christ. He met some very committed Christian business owners from all around the country who desired to lead their companies to honor Christ as well. He was one of the first, though, to make bold moves in how we did business in order to honor the Lord. Later, other owners followed his lead.

Usually, my two brothers needed more discipline than I did. But I went through my own ups and downs, became moody, adopted a "bad attitude," and ended up "butting heads" with my mom. That's when Dad would come in at night and just spend time with me, tickling my back and neck. As a result of his kindness, I grew out of that stage quickly and have become ever closer with my mother. In fact, I'm becoming more and more like her!

Since I married and became a pastor's wife, I've always had the best encouragement from Dad telling me how proud he is of me. I truly believe it has been a great blessing for my husband, Aaron, that I have such a close relationship with Dad. A father's love for his daughter does wonders for her ability to love and respect her husband.

It has always been such a blessing knowing that Dad wants to take care of my mom in every way. Even as he grows older and faces age-related challenges, he remains first and foremost concerned with her well-being. He shares with me his desire for the Pursell family to work together and live together on the farm. While that probably will not happen, we do love to gather all together around Dad and Mom whenever we can. He loves us all so much, he built a family cemetery on the farm so we all have a place to be remembered once we go home to heaven.

Dad has always loved being involved with many enterprises and activities, from Auburn University, to state and national politics, to health-related charities to help eradicate diseases such as diabetes and Alzheimer's and dementia. Above all, he has loved being a supporter of the local church, national and international Christian ministries, John Riley with The Path Foundation, and high school and collegiate ministries, such as the Fellowship of Christian Athletes. He is about the most generous man I've ever known. I pray that I will see that generosity continue through my dad and our family for many years to come.

APPENDIX 3

The Extrovert

BY DAVID PURSELL

When I was young, I remember how intrigued my father was with the family fertilizer business. Our daily routine involved first school and then stopping by the office afterward. My dad was a very hard worker, and it was a 24/7 thing with him. I never feared that the company would not prosper, mainly because of Dad's calm demeanor. He was always upbeat, especially around his children.

Family trips usually revolved around the business, as he would take advantage of meeting locations that were family-friendly. We were always introduced to customers and suppliers from an early age. I was taught to look adults in the eye and give a firm handshake. Jimmy Pursell seemed to know everybody and was held in high regard within the fertilizer industry.

Family

Dad has always loved Auburn, and he got me started very early on being an Auburn fan. He also started early modeling for me what it meant to be an "Auburn man." I remember going to football games with him on Saturdays back when Pat Sullivan and Terry Beasley were the stars. He even took me to my first Auburn versus Alabama football game in 1972. Alabama was dominating Auburn and led the game 16–3 with just a few minutes to go. Alabama was about to punt as we were walking out. Dad stopped us and asked me to watch just one more play. Auburn blocked the punt and ran it back for a touchdown, then repeated it two minutes later . . . and Auburn won the game! He and I were both acting like little kids as we walked out and drove home! Later, I would meet my future wife, Ellen, at Auburn, and we would have six children that would all attend and graduate from Auburn. We are definitely a War Eagle family!

I have an early memory of when he took me on my first hunting trip and let me shoot his shotgun for the first time. (Dad was really a novice hunter and didn't really prepare me for my first shot.) I put the stock of the gun *under* my arm, resting the back of the gun's barrel next to my nose. As I took a shot at a blackbird in a tree, the gun's hard recoil immediately bloodied my nose. I was crying, blood everywhere, but Dad kept insisting (to cheer me up) that I made a *great shot.* Still, I didn't shoot another shotgun for a few years after that.

Another family memory that I treasure is how my dad treated my mom. He always treated her like a lady—opening her door, allowing her to walk into a room first, holding her chair, not taking a bite before she did. He went out of his way to serve her. That was something I always wanted to do for my wife one day. He was also very committed to her, and they always seemed to be extremely happy together. They are the picture of a perfect marriage. I cannot emphasize enough what his example has meant to me, having now been married so many years!

Work

Dad gave all of the Pursell kids a chance to work and make a little money. He would always tell me, "Son, you have to earn your wings in the family business." *Nothing* was going to be given to us, and everything we made had to be earned.

My first job was a hot, sweaty one in a cottonseed warehouse with a pitchfork at age twelve. In the ginning business, the ginned cotton was baled and the cotton seed was blown in a pipe to an adjoining warehouse. My job was to move the piles from one side of the warehouse to the other; otherwise the hot piles of seed would catch fire. So, after school, I'd go to work and do what I could as a twelve year old for fifty cents per hour. My dad gave me the opportunity to work, and the work was not easy. Those early jobs were about learning what I *didn't* want to do the rest of my life! I appreciated the opportunity, though, and with the money, I could afford a few extra popsicles at school.

I was able to work in the family business all through high school, summers during college, and immediately after departing Auburn. Over the years, I was able to work with my father full-time from 1981 until today. He allowed me to be a part of making big decisions and even allowed me to make decisions myself. His support allowed me to run our controlled-release fertilizer business, to create Pursell Farms and FarmLinks golf course, and finally to sell the fertilizer business in 2006. We have made a pretty good team along the way!

Church

We attended church every Sunday at Saint Andrews Episcopal Church in Sylacauga. That is where I learned a reverence for God, but understanding the gospel more fully would come later. My dad would slip me a quarter to put in the offering, and sometimes it would make it in there, sometimes not! My brother and I became acolytes and learned to drink the cheap port wine they served for Communion.

My father and mother later had their own Christian conversion experience in the mid-1970s, ultimately resulting in a mutual decision to both give up drinking and smoking the same day. They were each other's accountability partner, and they have never gone back to those practices. They felt that smoking and drinking wielded too much control over their lives and reflected poorly on their Christian witness. Their decision was huge, since most all their personal friends and business associates were "partakers." At the time, it was a bold move that many people deeply respected.

Discipline

My mother was always the disciplinarian. If I got out of line, she would pull my ear, pull my hair, or dump a glass of cold water over my head. My dad would generally come home from work and everything was in order. I do remember a couple of times when we boys got our dad's ire up! Once, Taylor was doing some yard work (which we both had to do around the house each week) and Dad asked him a question, to which he replied with a sassy comment. The next thing I remember, Taylor was running from Dad (at the time, Taylor was a halfback on the high school football team) and Dad made a beautiful open-field tackle on him. He then proceeded to give the slower halfback a spanking.

Then there was the time when I was out by the highway with a friend, and when a car would come by, I would gesture as if I was about to jump out in front of the car. I'm not sure what I was thinking, but my dad caught a glimpse of what I was doing and immediately snatched me from the road and gave me that same spanking!

Chrissy was pretty much perfect and didn't seem ever to get into trouble with my parents! Spankings were a rarity, but when my father had to do it, he would. I think it was the lecture we'd get afterward that was the most effective. We respected our dad so much that we really didn't want to disappoint him.

Other Observations

My dad is one of the most outgoing people I have ever met. If a picture were to appear in the Webster's Dictionary by the word *extrovert*, it would be of my dad. To this day he never meets a stranger. He would always wave at everyone he would pass while driving around town. He truly never had any enemies.

He was and is a steady, committed family man and one of the most generous people I've ever met—even when we didn't have that much. I remember he would give the kids a share of Parker Fertilizer stock each year for Christmas, and we would not fully appreciate it. (We had friends whose fathers owned car dealerships, and they were getting new cars once a year!) It would not be until twenty-five years later that we realized the value of that stock!

My dad is also a straight-up, honest man. He would always do the right thing.

My father was quite a brilliant businessman, resulting in success all along his career—he always seemed to have the "Midas Touch." He had the right idea for the right time. Success followed him, but especially after he committed the family business to Christ. After that, he found success in nearly everything he did. If a man commits his way to the Lord, as the Scriptures teach, the Lord will direct his path. I saw that principle demonstrated in my dad's life every day.

My father has also given so much back to so many charitable entities, more than anyone can imagine. Though no man is perfect, he has been an almost-perfect role model for my siblings and me. No one could ask for a better father figure than the one we grew up with.